ANGELS IN THE ARCHITECTURE

ANGELS IN THE
ARCHITECTURE

A PROTESTANT VISION FOR MIDDLE EARTH

DOUGLAS JONES
DOUGLAS WILSON

canonpress
Moscow, Idaho

Published by Canon Press
P.O. Box 8729, Moscow, ID 83843
800–488–2034 | www.canonpress.com

Douglas Jones and Douglas Wilson,
Angels in the Architecture: A Protestant Vision for Middle Earth
Copyright © 1998 by Douglas Jones and Douglas Wilson

Unless otherwise indicated, all Scripture quotations are from the Authorized Version of the Bible.

Cover design by David Dalbey.
Interior design by Laura Storm.
Printed in the United States of America.

Library of Congress Cataloging-in-Publication Data

Jones, Douglas, 1963-
  Angels in the architecture : a Protestant vision for middle earth / Douglas Jones, Douglas Wilson.
      p. cm.
  ISBN-13: 978-1-885767-40-0 (pbk.)
  ISBN-10: 1-885767-40-4 (pbk.)
  1. Protestantism. 2. Medievalism. I. Wilson, Douglas, 1953- II. Title.
  BX4817.J66 2010
  270.3--dc22

                                    2009033557

10 11 12 13 14 15   9 8 7 6 5 4 3

CONTENTS

"It's medieval," I exclaimed; for I still had all the chronological snobbery of my period and used the names of earlier periods as terms of abuse.

C. S. Lewis

FOREWORD

BY GEORGE GRANT

It is a basic principle of spiritual integrity that only light can incarnate. In fact, according to Thomas Aquinas, only in radiance can truth, beauty, or goodness be known. Light—both physical and moral—was thus a central concern to the men and women living in the medieval age. They attempted to explore its properties in the colors of a stained glass canopy, in the tenor of a brisk saltarello, in the lilt of a jongleur's ballad, in the sweet savor of a banqueting table, in the rhapsody of a well planned garden, indeed, in every arena and discipline of life.

It is therefore more than a little ironic that their culture has commonly been described as the Dark Ages—as if the light of civilization had somehow been unceremoniously snuffed out for a time. It has similarly been dubbed the Middle Ages—as if it were a sort of gaping parenthesis in mankind's long upward march to modernity. It was in fact anything but dark or middling. Perhaps our greatest fault today is that we limit ourselves by a chronological parochialism. It is difficult for us to attribute anything but backwardness to those epochs and cultures that do not share our goals or aspirations.

The medieval period was actually quite remarkable for its many advances—perhaps unparalleled in all of history. It was a true *nascence,* while the epoch that followed was but a *re-nascence.* It was a new and living thing that gave flower to a culture marked by energy and creativity. From the monolithic security of Byzantium's imperias in the east to the reckless diversity of Christendom's fiefs in the west, it was a glorious crazy quilt of human fabrics, textures, and hues.

The titanic innovations medievalism brought forth were legion: it gave birth to all the great universities of the world from Oxford and Cambridge to Leipzig to Mainz; it oversaw the establishment of all the great hospitals of the world from St. Bartholomew's and Bedlam in London to St. Bernard's and Voixanne in Switzerland; it brought forth the world's most celebrated artists from Michelangelo Buonarroti and Albrecht Dürer to Leonardo da Vinci and Jan van Eyck; it gave us the splendor of Gothic architecture—unmatched and unmatchable to this day—from Notre Dame and Chartres to Winchester and Cologne; it thrust out into howling wilderness and storm-tossed seas the most accomplished explorers from Amerigo Vespucci and Marco Polo to Vasco da Gama and John Cabot; it produced some of the greatest minds and most fascinating lives mankind has yet known— were the list not so sterling it might begin to be tedious— Copernicus, Dante, Giotto, Becket, Gutenberg, Chaucer, Charlemagne, Wyclif, Magellan, Botticelli, Donatello, Petrarch, and Aquinas.

But of all the great innovations that medievalism wrought, the greatest of all was spiritual. Medieval culture—both east and west—was first and foremost Christian culture. Its life was shaped almost entirely by Christian concerns. Virtually all of its achievements were submitted to the cause of the Gospel. From great cathedrals and gracious chivalry to bitter crusades and beautiful cloisters, every manifestation of its presence was somehow tied to its utter and complete obeisance to Christ's kingdom and to the pursuit of beauty, truth, and goodness.

Of course, the medieval church had its share of dangerous and scandalous behavior. It had gross libertines and rank heretics. It had false professors and bold opportunists. It had brutal ascetics and imbalanced tyrants. But then, there was no more of that sort of rank heterodoxy than we have today in our Evangelical and Reformed circle. As a result, medievalism was forever a paradox. It was a romantic riddle. On the one hand it was marked by the greatest virtues of morality, charity, and selflessness; on the other hand it was marred by the flaming vices of perversity, betrayal, and avarice. It was often timid, monkish, and isolated; more often still, it was bold, ostentatious, and adventurous. It was mystical; it was worldly. It was tender-hearted; it was cruel. It was ascetic; it was sensual. It was miserly; it was pretentious. It gripped men with a morbid superstition; it set them free with an untamed inquisitiveness. It exulted in pomp, circumstance, and ceremony; it cowered in poverty, tyranny, and injustice. It united men with faith, hope, and love; it divided them with war, pestilence, and prejudice. It was so unstable it could hardly have been expected to last a week; it was so stable that it actually lasted a millennium.

The contrast with our own culture is stark. And that contrast is really what this remarkable book of essays is about. Exploring various themes of aesthetics, dogmatic theology, sociology, and domesticity. Douglas Wilson and Douglas Jones have thrown into high relief the dramatic differences between the vivid and lively world of medievalism and the dim and dreary world of modernity.

In very practical, though elegant terms, they have afforded us a rare perspective of the Christian worldview. Whenever the subject of worldview comes up, we Protestants—and especially we Reformed Protestants—typically think of philosophy. And that is really too bad. We think of intellectual niggling. We think of theological lint picking. We think of the brief and blinding oblivion of ivory tower speculation, of thickly obscure tomes, and of inscrutable logical complexities. In fact, a worldview is as practical as garden arbors, public manners, whistling at work, dinner-time rituals, and architectural angels. It is less metaphysical than understanding marginal market buying at the stock exchange or legislative initiatives in congress. It is less esoteric than typing a book into a laptop computer or sending a fax across the continent. It is instead, Wilson and Jones assert, as down to earth as inculcating a culture-wide appetite for beauty, truth, and goodness.

In the midst of a world seemingly gone mad, *Angels in the Architecture* demonstrates that this peculiarly biblical worldview has actually been lived out before—however imperfectly, by the medievals who have gone before us. It simultaneously holds out the promise that it may actually be lived out once again. Thus, it gives us a hopeful vision of a once and future age of light. And for that, we can all be thankful.

Homer once sang of his Hellenes and Trojans
and Vergil composed verse about the descendants
    of Romulus;
Let us sing about the kindly deeds of the king
    of Heaven
whom the world never ceases joyously to praise.
Homer and Vergil took pleasure in speaking about
    the flames that brought
sudden destruction to Troy and about the struggles
    of their heroes,
but our delight is to sing of Christ
drenched in blood after vanquishing the prince of
    this world.
They were both learned in how to compose
    falsehoods
with an appearance of truth and how to deceive an
    Arcadian verse;
we prefer to sing hymns of fine praise
to the power of the Father and His true wisdom.
Let us therefore hold the supreme victories of Christ
as brilliant stars in our minds.
Behold the four corners of the world are clasped by
    the wooden cross.

John Scotus (A.D. 810–877)

CHAPTER 1

INTRODUCTION: POSITIVELY MEDIEVAL

Modernity or medievalism? That is admittedly an odd choice, and it is the topic of this admittedly odd book. But at our place in history it appears to be the only choice before us. History has shown us all the options—nothing is fresh, and everything "new" either fades away or turns out to be just another shadow of modernity. This book aims to answer the question above by defending the impossible—Christian medievalism.

The colors of the essays to follow may not seem to blend together at first glance. They mix such topics as poetry, predestination, and plowshares, with highlights of justification, wine, and lovemaking. We aim to sketch a vision of a whole life and a whole culture, and such things are always a broad landscape of hues. The trick is to realize how these various issues intermingle quite smoothly. We see them as a warm harmony of color, and if the reader grasps the same, then we've accomplished one of our hopes.

Though this sort of effort may appear frivolous to moderns, we will try to show through our trail of essays that such a fleshing out of the Christian gospel is *terribly* central for day-to-day Christian living. Nothing should hold our attention more. Nothing is more practical.

Modernity's empire has dominated the world for only three centuries, even though the soul of the modern vision is that of the meat cleaver's counter: stainless steel—cold and functional and sterile, with efficient smears of blood. Modernity is a busy place, spinning with silicon speed that goes ever faster but never forward, people pressed into cities full of loneliness. "There's got to be an opening somewhere here in front of me / Through this maze of ugliness and greed / I'm so alone, I feel just like somebody else."

Modernity and its natural child postmodernity are pleased with their rejection of truth, beauty, and goodness—the three faces of culture. In their place, they unfold the tired, wrinkled banners of a tedious rationalism and socially-just sentimentalism. But the modern void is a vacuum. Real beauty has no place to sit; Darwin has locked the door. Yet moderns don't give up the game. Their prophets stand stage-tall, throw out law, yet condemn injustice, trashing simple oaths for new, unridden flesh.

Each sharp-eyed generation tires of everything except their joy of rebellion, playing it over and over again, in an endless roll. Everything is boring except their own eternal rebellion. This is their totally "new and different program for the future." This is modernity's barbarism—hollow hearts led about by sterile matter, perversely mocking those with full lives.

This modern, Enlightenment story will be with us for at least another century, crushing and infiltrating and absorbing its opponents. All will fall—Islamic swords, New Age whining, and Roman Catholic hierarchies. Modernity's vision subverts its opponents best by just turning on a television in the midst of an unsuspecting culture; leave it on and soon Muslims and Hindus will come to love Star Trek and Seinfeld more than Allah and Brahman. And despite postmodernism's annoying little requiem over modernity, it is postmodernism that will be a tiny epicycle within the history of modernism. The relativists and sophists have always shown up for short apocalyptic spasms within the history of philosophy, only to fade out before they could be included in the history books. Sophists, ancient or postmodern, have no staying power because they tell an ugly story, all while using the rationalists' tools. They rarely need refuting; in the end they usually just fade from the stage when their once sexy story produces yawns. That is happening now.

So the future is either with modernity or Christian medievalism. But why medievalism and not just vanilla evangelicalism? Modern evangelicalism is just that—modern—in love with modernity, in love with individualism, egalitarianism, and perfect boxes. Like other moderns, evangelicals have no love of beauty; it is at most optional and indifferent, not the rhythm of life.

Christian medievalism, however, presents us with a view of a whole life, full of truth, beauty, goodness and all their nasty contraries. *The medieval period is the closest thing we have to a maturing Christian culture.* It was a culture unashamed of Christ and one sharply at odds with the values of modernity. Where else can Christians look for a vision of normal life, of Christianity enfleshed? Do we look to the 1950's? Life on the American prairie? To Jefferson's reign? Modernism had already gutted Christian culture long before any of these.

To the Reformation? That period was a crucial outgrowth of medievalism, but it was a period of crass and heroic trauma, of emergency living. It was a time to focus on truth amidst a slaughterhouse—abnormal—but it would be a great mistake to try to make emergencies the model of a culture, as too many in the Reformed community, our community, do—like Cold Warriors twitching over the launch buttons after the enemy has closed shop. The Reformation was real war, and we dare not give up the victories gained there, but how do we live after the nightly air raids have stopped? That is the vision of *Medieval Protestantism*—a view that picks up the discussion where medievalism was silenced by a tyrannical Rome and a blinding Enlightenment.

Medieval Protestantism is certainly not a longing to live in medieval times and wear their funny hats. It's an attempt to continue that Christian discussion of truth, beauty, and goodness that was cut so short. The medieval period is not the culmination of Christian culture, but it was headed in the right direction. It was telling a wonderful story and headed for great things, triumphing with beauty over its enemies. But it never got to complete the story. Christians need to start thinking more about plotting the rest of that story, preparing for the death of modernity over the next century. It's time to renew our devotion to Christian truth, beauty, and goodness—the good life. But in order to continue that discussion, we need to search out how our medieval forefathers were progressing before they were silenced. We need to learn to scoff at modernity's tired idols and examine the many levels of the medieval Christian vision—"ask for the old paths, where is the good way, and walk therein, and ye shall find rest for your souls" (Jer. 6:16).

When we look into the "old paths" of our medieval fathers to find rest for our souls, it is like finding long lost family, family we've been severed from for centuries. We find them to be brothers, refreshingly Christian and unaddicted to modern idols. We want to kiss them and ask where they have been for such a long time (rather, where have we been?). They have their foibles and idols, just as we have ours, but we can learn.

When we commune with medieval thinking we learn to see how silly modern project is, and we can start to understand why modernity hates medievalism. It cannot speak about it without going red in the face. Modernity's hatred of all things medieval should be reason enough for Christians to desire it. After all, if modernity hates medievalism so much, there must be something wonderful there. During C. S. Lewis's slow trek out of modernism, he noticed how one Christian professor "was beginning to overthrow [Lewis's] chronological snobbery. Had something really dropped out of our lives? Was the archaic simply the civilized, and the modern simply the barbaric?" Christendom has lost something beautiful. Barbarism has always been with us, yet Christendom once held forth a life full of truth, beauty, and goodness amidst barbarism.

Given the choice between modernism and Medieval Protestantism, how shall we decide? Many strategies have gone before us. But why not judge the respective visions by their beauty? Which vision tells the better story? Which has poetic grace and rich color? Most of us realize the legitimate place of syllogisms and rational grounds. But the rational rarely satisfies even modernists. Pascal explained that "every man is almost always led to believe not through proof, but through that which is attractive. This way is low, unworthy and alien, and so everyone refuses to acknowledge it." All of us are led on by beauty. Pascal thinks that is base, but it seems to be the way God designed us. We can never know enough arguments to be omniscient, but we can judge fruit. And beauty is fruit.

Why are we so confident that beauty isn't a path to truth? More modern lies I suspect. Scripture tells us that God beautifies a people by salvation (Ps. 149:4) and that holiness itself is beautiful (Ps. 29:2). If beauty points us to salvation and holiness, then beauty points us to truth. Idolatry can never be *truly* beautiful. Non-Christians will dismiss the challenge, but they have to because modernism is so ugly. The more important judgment needs to be made by modern Christians. Compare medievalism to our baptized modernity. Which is more beautiful? This is a key to truth. Or even to lower the standard: wouldn't it be wonderful *if* the medieval vision were true? That is the concern in a discussion of Medieval Protestantism. Of course, we advocates don't pretend to do any justice in describing the beauty of the medieval vision, warped as we are by our own modern upbringing; but we can enjoy the beauty of the vision itself. Modernity and Medieval Protestantism—compare the beauty. Just imagine for a moment that the medieval vision is true. How beautiful life would be! "O taste and see that the LORD is good: blessed is the man that trusteth in him" (Ps. 34:8).

In addition, Pascal's observation should give us hope. If beauty is the deepest persuasive, and a full-fleshed Christianity—Medieval Protestantism—is the most beautiful vision of reality, of the good life, then modernity has to fail and medievalism has to triumph in middle earth—"Let the beauty of the Lord our God be upon us, and establish thou the work of our hands upon us" (Ps. 90:17).

But what about our use of the phrase *middle earth?* In one sense, we are referring to the traditional cosmology of the earth being suspended between heaven and hell. We are using it, however, in another sense too, a sense based on an ancient tie in the history of the two words. Even if we cannot make the etymological case, then we can use it as an etymological illustration. The English word *earth* comes from the same Old English word that gives us *yard*, a tamed piece of ground. In this sense, think of *middle earth* as a cultivated portion of land, surrounded by wilderness. The wilderness is modernity, full of monsters, and the yard is a small and pleasant shire. While our children are little, we want to imitate our medieval forefathers and tell our children the truths in fairy tales that will keep them out of the woods. When they are grown, they will be able to fight the monsters and expand the fences of middle earth.

What are the features, then, which make up Medieval Protestantism? The best way to grasp them is to immerse oneself in medieval literature. King Alfred and Charlemagne reveal to us magnificent struggles in the high and late middle ages. Consider Boccaccio's *Decameron* (selectively and discerningly) for its enjoyment of life and honor, Dante's *Divine Comedy* for the best poetry, and especially Langland's *Piers Plowman* for a feel of the late medieval loves and worries. Through these and so much more we find all the elements of a Medieval Protestantism, elements we try to lay out in the following pages, namely a love of beauty, an Augustinian appreciation for the sovereignty of God, the chasm between pagan and Christian, the centrality of laughter, the importance of celebration, a covenantal wholeness of family and society, a submissive hierarchicalism, respect for good traditions, sphere sovereignty, anti-papalism, a harmonization of technology and humanity, an agrarian calm, disciplined silence, the glory of a unified Holy Church, a skepticism of novelty, and a triumphant, peaceful hope for the future of Christendom.

The Reformation was in many ways a continuation of a theological discussion of authority, worship, and redemption which had been started in the middle ages, and the early Protestants were far more medieval than modern. Consequently, the Protestant concerns were medieval concerns, and the two fit together organically, naturally. The supreme authority of Scripture and the unspeakable joy of imputed righteousness rest comfortably with the medieval celebration of life, a life full of beauty, tradition, community, laughter, and celebration. But this still is only a flat list. The discussion sits largely in dusty books in countless libraries.

Medieval Protestantism is not a call to a movement, another one of those tiresome modern constructs of strategies and polemics. It is a call for meditation and living out the good life one family at a time. We so often talk of "worldview thinking" and "applying the Bible to every area of life," but that is all too often just a skeleton of a theory. The medievals actually lived it; imperfectly, yes, but still much better than anything in modernity. We have no sense of a life carefully crafted by beauty. A devotion to beauty will sculpt everything we do, and the medievals knew that very well. Beauty trains one's mind to think differently about family, leisure, labor, theology, and the future. Yet we thin-souled moderns are so proud of our rejection of poems and stories and paintings. We lead half-lives and die with less. God has given us so much more, and we slight Him in our meager living. Christendom has lost so much. Christendom has lost Christendom, and we have traded middle earth away for cold and sterile idols.

A WINE DARK SEA AND TUMBLING SKY

RETURNING TO THE LOVE OF BEAUTY

Too late came I to love thee, O thou Beauty
both so ancient and so fresh . . .

—Augustine of Hippo

The holiness of God is not so much a distinct attribute as it is the manifestation of all His attributes in all their splendor. As the color white is not a separate color, but rather all colors together, so the seraphim acknowledge all the attributes of God in their great *triagion*.

When the prophets and apostles turn to describe this holiness, it is remarkable that they do not use phrases like the "kindness of holiness," or the "goodness of holiness." When called upon to speak concerning what holiness is like, they overwhelmingly speak of the *beauty* of holiness. Modernity has come to think of beauty as being relative to the individual, whether artist or observer. It is thought to be something which wells up from within each individual in what we are pleased to call the creative process. The artist is one who expresses himself; he is an autonomous font of art and creativity. Instinctively we do know that true beauty proceeds only from Deity. Our problem is that we have deified ourselves and have assumed, contrary to the visible results, that whatever proceeds from us must be beautiful.

But in a created world, beauty can only be reflected glory. Our world is filled with moons, and there is only one sun. As much as we would like the aesthetic process to be originative, as much as we would like to be as God and create *ex nihilo*, we are left with the fact that mere man is not much; his breath is in his nostrils. In order to recover a sense of the beautiful, we must come to see it in connection with the two other great questions—"What is true?" and "What is good?" When these are answered in a fashion consistent with the way the created world *is*, we may then with profit consider "What is beauty?"

Theology is seen by us as a dry and dreary pursuit, conducted by scholars who, to use a phrase of Keats, cough in ink. Almost no one thinks of the seraphim as theologians. No one assumes that the twenty-four elders before the throne are an assembly of divines. But when the Apostle Paul finished working through one of the most complex theological arguments in all Scripture, he signified his understanding by bursting into doxological praise: "Oh, the depth of the riches both of the wisdom and knowledge of God!" A true theologian, he loved beauty.

Sound theology leads always to the love of beauty. When there is no love of beauty, we may say, reasoning *modus tollens*, that there is no sound theology. Now the logic of the thing can also mean that wrangles about theology may certainly lead to wrangles about aesthetics. But this is not our purpose here. We do not seek out ugly disputes about the nature of beauty. Our point is simply that a love for the triune and holy God is the foundation of any true love for beauty. Like the seraphim, we do not see this beauty directly, for our faces, like theirs, are of necessity covered. But the fact that this beauty is infinitely *there* means that other entities in this created world can reflect it, and we have the privilege to behold the beauty of the Lord in them.

Moses, the man of God, certainly knew this. He cried out for a restoration of God's people, as do we. We who live at the nether end of modernity, with its sterile and technocratic ugliness, instinctively know this. We also see that, in a futile reaction to the ugliness of modernity, postmodernists have turned to the chaos of full relativism, hoping to recover some sense of humane beauty there. All of it is futile. In our folly, we do not know how to number our days, and we do not know how to apply our hearts to wisdom. The spirit of the age has enveloped the Christian church as well, and we look in vain toward contemporary evangelicalism for any reflection or sense of the beatific vision.

So the work of our hands is singularly unblessed. The Church, compromised by modernity, and in a hollow reaction to it, does little more aesthetically than manufacture pious kitsch. When reformation comes, we may, like Moses, ask God to bless and establish the work of our hands. But Moses knew what we do not—that this blessing would be the direct result of the Lord's efficacious beauty. "And let the beauty of the Lord our God be upon us: and establish thou the work of our hands upon us; yea, the work of our hands establish thou it" (Ps. 90:17).

When the psalmist comes before the Lord to worship, desiring to dwell in the Lord's house all the days of his life, it is in order that he might behold the beauty of the Lord (Ps. 27). Those who come before Him are to give the glory due His name; they are to come before him in the beauty of holiness (1 Chron. 16:29; Ps. 29:2; 110:3). The garments of Aaron were for glory and for beauty (Exod. 28:2). The beauty of God's holiness is itself an object of praise (2 Chron. 20:21).

God shines from His people, the perfection of beauty (Ps. 50:2). Honor and majesty befit the Lord; strength and beauty adorn His sanctuary (Ps. 96:6–9). All these references to beauty are related in some fashion to the holiness of God, which in turn describe all that He is. This being the case, the question of beauty should be of much greater concern to us than it is.

But the modern evangelical either says that our aesthetic vision should be borrowed from the world, or in reaction, says that since we must not borrow from the world, we must be content with no beauty at all. We divide between those who say that our beauty must be in accord with contemporary trends and follies and those who say we must not compromise with beauty of any kind. Both positions miss the clear scriptural vision, and both agree to a central lie, which is that the world is the source of aesthetic wisdom and understanding. They do part company in their discussion whether or not to borrow this beauty, but they agree that the world originates what we in the Church do not.

The only possible conclusion is that the Church has forgotten the holiness of her God. He alone is true, and He alone is good. If we understood this, we would understand how beautiful His holiness is, and we could not be kept from writing concertos and building cathedrals. As it is, we are content with thumping on the guitar like a million other aspiring artists headed for Nashville, and we erect crystal cathedrals which look like an upscale gas works.

But the only possible beauty we may have is that of the Lord. The Lord is to be a crown of glory and diadem of beauty (Is. 28:5), and if He is not, then the beauty is not. He and only He is able to give beauty for ashes, with the result being His glory (Is. 61:3). When Job comes to a right mind, it is in part a humble response to God's sarcastic invitation to try to make his own private moon into a sun. "Deck thyself now with majesty and excellency; and array thyself with glory and beauty" (Job 40:10). And Job stopped his mouth, abashed.

When we have remembered who God is, we may then be in a position to remember the beauty of His conquest of history through the victory of Christ. For aeons we have sung of arms and men. The deeds sung were mighty, and the exploits of these masters were great. We have long sung of men like Odysseus and Aeneas, not only because they were clever, or pious, but because of the weight and beauty carried in the words of their chroniclers. But another triumph, another conquest, although accomplished and acknowledged, has not yet been sung as it deserves to be. The epic has not yet been written which tells of the greatest conquest in history, the conquest of history and all it contains, including that which is beautiful. When the devil offered our Lord the kingdoms of this world, *and the glory of them,* the Lord refused him. But this was done, not because He didn't want these kingdoms, but because He did not want them as a gift from the devil. His intention was to bind the strong man and take the beautiful plunder.

The older pagan beauty baffles us. We know that the *pietas* of a pagan was offered to demons, and we wonder to think that any man could be capable of offering such glories to the twisted. But in many cases these ancient men were simply offering back what had been given to them. The source of their aesthetic powers was not something which they sought to hide from us. In their glorious poetry and in all their art, they exhibited their devotion, calling upon the daughters of Zeus and Mnemosyne, the Muses, to fill their sails. And so the inspiration came, enrapturing the ancient artists and enabling them to produce works of unbelievable beauty. It baffles still. The splendor of these powers was imparted to men in the midst of a rebellious squalor. As C. S. Lewis observed, the granite despair of Homer was brought to shine like marble. And the ancient piety of Aeneas was fashioned as a diadem to adorn the head of a beast.

Modernity is amused by it all. We suppose that ancient and superstitious tomfooleries have been revealed as such by reason and science. But the apostle had a sharper view; he was never one to beat the air. His fight was against principalities, powers, and the wickedness which was everywhere present; the pagan world was *animate*. But still, all these ancient powers have fallen to the ground. Hosea knew the names of the baals would be taken from the mouths of men, to be remembered by name no more. Through the triumph of the Christian faith, all the elder powers and lords have been taken away. "And hear ancestral Muses cry the wine dark sea and tumbling sky."

Our Lord came in order to make His blessings flow as far as the curse could be found. Like a warrior in one of the old stories, He fell upon the adversary. The strong man was bound; his house was sacked like Troy. Only folly would return to that house, thinking to find any treasure there now. The treasure has been taken away and is now numbered among countless trophies in the house of the Lord. We may indeed boast when we remember there was a time when *we* were taken into exile, and all the articles from our Temple were taken away with us, and set up in an unholy city. Our music then was desolate as well, and our harps silent on the willows. Now, in the goodness of God, the situation is turned on itself; back in the sunlight, we may pour our libations to the Most High with golden cups which once were raised idolatrously in the dark places.

When our race was in its nonage, the Lord was pleased to number the sons of men and their nations according to the number of the celestials. When the Most High divided the nations, when He separated the sons of Adam, He set the bounds of the nations according to the number of the angels of God. We were governed, as children often are, by these nurses and tutors. Some of them, like Michael the prince, served the Lord at this station in humility. Others ruled with cruelty and hatred, murderers from the very beginning. The cherub of Tyre once walked on the holy mountain of God until iniquity was found in him. The power of Babylon was once a son of morning until he vaunted himself as God. The prince of Persia withstood the servants of the Lord and was later supplanted by the prince of Greece. The power of Ekron was lord of the flies and grew in power to become the lord of Rome. In the temptation of our Lord, this great devil was willing to give all his kingdoms away if our Lord would only bow down to him. But there was no need to receive as a gift what was soon to be taken as spoil in battle.

While the goodness of all our Lord's adversaries had vanished away with their initial rebellion, their splendor had not. This splendor was imparted by them in various ways to the sons of men, but Christ came in order to take *that* kind of splendor away from us. His purpose in this was to establish another kind of glory in its place, the beauty of holiness.

We may say with gratitude and humility that the purpose of God in history is to redeem the world and to bring mankind up to maturity in Christ. What is man? And yet God has been pleased to set all things under his feet. We were created to make beautiful things—in music, in stone, on canvas, in sculpted gardens, and in wonderful buildings. But because of our rebellion in Adam, we not only fell away from our appointed task, we also fell under the tutelage of cruel masters. The ground quickly filled with thorns, and the sky was filled with malevolence. And so we were rudely governed, like disobedient children. The splendor of that ancient world was not fully human. The ancient boast that man is the measure of all things was made by those who had an alliance with another realm, and that realm was not a kingdom of *men*.

Our Lord was born as one of us in order to redeem us and topple all these ancient powers. As that great aeon came crashing to a close, the pillars holding that old sky were thrown down; a new heaven and new earth were established. The seed of David came to destroy the one who had the power of death, that is, the devil. When He was lifted up in death, at that moment the ruler of that age was cast down. And when He had triumphed over all these powers, He made a spectacle of them, taunting and humiliating them. The governors of that aeon were overthrown, and in the wisdom of God it was accomplished through their murder of a righteous Man. Clearly, if the rulers of that age had known what they were doing, they would never have crucified our Lord and our glory.

Authority was wrested from them and turned over to man. Not man in Adam, and not man under guardians, but man in Christ. Now God's wisdom is exhibited in . . . mere men. The manifold wisdom of God was set before the celestials, and it was set before them in the church—that is, man in Christ. Certainly we do not yet see everything in subjection to man, but we are instructed to see Christ. And as more and more of us see Him, we will also see the cultural fruit of seeing Him. Since the kingdoms of men were first shaken to the ground and replaced with a kingdom that cannot be shaken, we have seen wonderful things. The advances in theology, architecture, painting, confessions, philosophy, literature, and music have been considerable; as His kingdom continues to grow, we may expect to see what eye has not yet seen. Our wisdom is not from the rulers of that age, who came to nothing. God's ordained wisdom cannot fall to the ground; it was established before the ages for our glory. Eye has not seen and ear has not heard the coming beauty given by grace. Of the increase of His government there will be no end.

As with all other spheres, God governs our progress in aesthetics by degrees. The destruction of the old culture, and the institution of the new, was not accomplished instantaneously. The rock which struck the great king's statue grew to fill the earth. The mustard seed grew; the full-grown tree was not lowered to us from the heavens. Because Jesus is Lord, Christian culture is now established in the earth. But He does not want to do everything for us all at once. The powers fell in an instant, but the cultures they supported took more time to fall. The unbelievers have not been driven out all at once lest the beasts of the field turn on us.

And whenever a great city falls, the dust and rubble must be removed before anything can be done. When the saints overthrew Jericho, the inhabitants were slain, but the treasures preserved. After the Lord's triumph, the rubble of that ancient world took considerable time to remove—and many treasures had to be brought out to be built into the new city—and this slow process still annoys the impatient. But now, as always, in patience we possess our souls.

Many proud moderns still do not like to admit their complete dependence on Christ, and they will certainly resent it when the glory and beauty of culture is attributed to Him. But splendid pagan culture is really no longer a historical possibility—the Muses are gone. Any culture which desires beauty now must have the beauty of holiness. Christ is Lord of all now; He is certainly the Lord of beauty. When the travesties scattered throughout our modern art museums are set alongside the glories of ancient Greece, the Christian heart should swell with pride. Our Lord has thrown unbelievers down, and they can never recover. Look at what they now do on their own! The modern materialist has truly fallen between two stools—he cannot have the Nike of Samothrace, and he cannot have Bach's Mass in B Minor. He cannot have Vergil and he cannot have Milton. But he can hang a toilet seat on the gallery wall and apply for federal grants—we are all just prisoners here of our own device.

Modern man has not had beauty taken away from him; but in order to have beauty, it must now be borrowed in the context of Christian culture. This means that in repentance he must now turn away from both modernity and postmodernity. Although unbelievers may still produce works of great beauty, they are dependent upon Christian culture as they do so. Turning from our Lord Christ means turning from the only fountainhead of true aesthetic wonder.

The apostle saw in his vision that the kings of the earth would bring their glory into the new Jerusalem. So a glorious future awaits, and a great part of that glory is the glory found in beautiful things. We must consider by faith the beauty that remains yet to be brought into the world, and which, in the centuries to come, will be brought into the Church. Eye has not seen . . . but perhaps the eye of faith can make something out.

Over time the church will continue to mature in Christ and teach the meaning of loveliness to an unbelieving world. Not only so, but she will also exhibit a vision of loveliness to the world. As the saints are equipped to serve Christ in everything they do, their works will glorify Him. This will, of course, happen in law and auto mechanics, but it will also happen in the library and studio, with the pen and brush. The distance between Odysseus and Beowulf was great, but the distance between Beowulf and the works to come will be greater still. Charlemagne was a lesser king than Darius, but he was also a different sort of king. God has been very kind to us.

Regardless of these great works of Christ, unbelief is always content to walk along, looking at the ground. And admittedly we live in a time when the church has tired of her assigned task of pointing up at the kingdom of heaven—for the last century or so the church has failed to instruct believers on their duty of glorifying God through beauty. We were told to be salt and light for everything men do, including the realm of the arts. But because we are currently occupied in our manufacture of cutesy porcelain figurines, the world has been left to turn aside to aesthetic chaos. They have done so, and so we must take the long view. Disobedience in the church does not take Christ off His throne any more than disobedience anywhere else. Of the increase of His government there will be no end. "Exalt and sing the Lord on high, of wine dark sea and tumbling sky."

The days to come will be glorious.

> And the Lord their God shall save them in that day as the flock of his people: for they shall be as the stones of a crown, lifted up as an ensign upon his land. For how great is his goodness, and how great is his beauty! Corn shall make the young men cheerful, and new wine the maids. (Zech. 9:16–17)

TE DEUM

"Nobody," she said, "would doubt that God is all powerful."

"At any rate," said I, "no sane man would doubt it."

—Boethius

When the referent is the living God, words quickly come to the end of their tether. Our words are creatures, just as we are, and as such they cannot really express the ineffable. When we are speaking of God, no word *encapsulates*. No creature can draw a boundary which successfully circumscribes any one of His attributes. To say this is nothing more than to admit our creaturely limitations. We were created *imago Dei*, and the words we have been given carry the same limitations.

Some have used this as a basis for objecting to the use of all such attempted descriptions, but such an approach leads directly to the swamps of mysticism. Words like *sovereign, almighty, omnipotent* are thought to be too restrictive—they are too tiny to express truth about God fully. This is quite right; they are too small, but the solution is certainly not to be found by opting for *smaller* words. That would be nothing but a rebellious revolt against heaven. And the option of *no* words is not feasible either. To refuse *any* verbal descriptions of God is to rebel against the very idea of Scripture, not to mention how it sets aside the duties assigned to us in Scripture. We are commanded to declare His praises and to embrace the futility of the task.

> Many, O Lord my God, are thy wonderful works which thou hast done, and thy thoughts which are to us-ward: they cannot be reckoned up in order unto thee: if I would declare and speak of them, they are more than can be numbered. (Ps. 40:5)

When we sing "Immortal, invisible, God only wise," only a fool would think to set the hymnal aside after the first verse because he has exhausted the subject.

These limits apply equally to those words which God Himself has given us in order to reveal Himself. God has spoken to us about Himself in Scripture, and we must hold that these self-descriptions are perfect. But if the limits apply, perfect in what sense? "The voice of thy thunder was in the heaven: the lightnings lightened the world: the earth trembled and shook" (Ps. 77:18). We affirm that this is so, and yet God is much greater than Thor. Thunder can be adequately described by a meteorologist. So how can thunder be used to communicate truth about God? The same basic question rises up with any of God's attributes. "Alleluia: for the Lord God omnipotent reigneth" (Rev. 19:6). God is the all-powerful One, but how are we as finite creatures to understand the infinitude of the *all*?

Scholastic theologians rescue us from this impasse by teaching us to get used to it. Knowledge of God is necessarily analogical. The attributes of God—*attributa divina*—cannot be apprehended fully by any creature. No created intellect can conceive of a single word suitable for God's most infinite and simple essence. Any word we use to describe God will quickly fall to the ground exhausted—like us, our words fall short of the glory of God. But this does not mean that the use of such words is pointless. We must say that God is holy and sovereign, but we must also exercise due caution. This caution means that we must constantly remind ourselves that we do not have this holiness in a box; we do not have His sovereignty cupped in our hands. We must say *this is the truth about God*, but then point beyond the truth to much more.

One alternative to obedience is to say that He is less than holy, or unholy, and not really sovereign over everything. The problem with this is immediately evident. Or we could remain silent on the point, refusing to say anything about His attributes one way or the other for fear of being misleading. We might be especially tempted to this when we see ignorant people mouthing words about sovereignty and power and glory while assuming they understand the full extent of what they say. But to say nothing yields far more to them than is lawful. Our words about God must be true, and carefully selected. We must not be put off by those who use glorious words without understanding. A godly response would be to reject the folly of self-sufficiency, not the words which point necessarily away from self-sufficiency.

We must speak of God, and we must speak of Him truly. In His grace and mercy, He does not require us to speak of Him exhaustively. A good place to learn this lesson is from the poets. When using poetry we are most clear on the point. God's providences are traced upon our dial by the Sun of love. We take the royal diadem to crown Him Lord of all. Our God is a fortress, a bulwark never-failing. And as Langland said, pointing helplessly at the mercy of God, "all the wickedness in this world that man might work or think is no more to the mercy of God than a live coal in the sea."

When we are using formal theological language, we are most tempted to forget ourselves, thinking that theologians are the engineers of the divine attributes, and they have a schematic diagram for everything about Him. But they do not, and the theologians who are wise will frequently say so. Properly understood, the formal descriptions we give of God are not boundaries for the divine essence; they are the well-marked boundaries between creaturely knowledge and creaturely ignorance. When we heed them, it leads us to true knowledge, a knowledge which ends in worship. Bede (A.D. 673–735) records how Cædmon praised the Lord, even in his sleep:

> Now we must praise the Maker of the heavenly kingdom, the power of the Creator and His counsel, the deeds of the Father of glory and how He, since He is the eternal God, was the Author of all marvels and first created the heavens as a roof for the children of men and then, the almighty Guardian of the human race, created the earth.

Another example of the vastness of the medieval conception of God can be taken from the poetic fringes of the medieval world—the world of the barbarian north. This was a world just emerging from heathenism, and so the conception of God came from the more civilized south. Imagine yourself standing on the shores of the North Sea, with the sky above you cold and pale. Your father, or perhaps your grandfather, had been a loyal pagan servant of Thor and Odin. You, like them, are both noble and barbaric, but, unlike them, you are Christian. The emergence of your house from heathenism is recent, and apostasy an ever present possibility, as the Danes once showed by falling back into the worship of their devils. But you and your people, the Geats of southern Sweden, still stand delivered. You look at your ship, which is *isig ond utfus,* covered with ice and ready to sail. You are ready to embark, and look out over the *hrond-rode*, or whale road. You live in a cold and austere world, but one full of a glittering and severe beauty.

C. S. Lewis once spoke of the lure of pagan "north-ernness," a lure which in turn was used to help draw him to Christ. "Pure 'Northernness' engulfed me; a vision of huge, clear spaces hanging above the Atlantic in the endless twilight of Northern summer, remoteness, severity."[1] This northernness is not necessarily Christian, but when turned to Christ, it is redeemed like all sinful things and stands upright. But we moderns have little interest in such redemp-tions or their results because the Church in our era is slack and effeminate. We do not look at an unbounded northern sky and by analogy see the eternity of God; rather, we look mystically inward to the swamps and standing puddles of our own hearts and see just what one might expect in such places—but not very much and not very far.

At the bottom of this contrast, indeed, at the bottom of every contrast, is the view taken of God. For example, the outlines of the *Beowulf* story are fascinating, and the anony-mous Anglian poet who wrote it in the eighth century was clearly a Christian speaking to well-instructed Christians. One of his virtues as a poet was that he could clearly re-member when his people had not been in the faith. We may recall that the Lord Jesus rebukes the Ephesians for falling from their first love. Individualists as we are, we commonly apply this admonition only to individuals whose love and individual zeal flags over the individual course of their in-dividual lives. But what of cultures? What was it like for us when our scattered tribes first came to Christ? How did we

1. C. S. Lewis, *Surprised by Joy* (New York: Harcourt, Brace & World, Inc., 1955), 73.

think of the Almighty then? And how do we see Him now in our supposed urbane and modern sophistication?

In the course of the story, Beowulf kills both Grendel and Grendel's mother, descendents of Cain. A humble man, Beowulf the great warrior gives glory to God. He rules as a king of his people for many years, and does not fall into an overweening pride the way many other Viking chieftains fell. At the end of the book, in his old age, he fights and kills a great dragon and loses his life in the conflict. In that fight with the dragon, the number of Beowulf's retainers is the same number as Christ's disciples, and, like the disciples, they also scatter. Many other parallels throughout the poem make Beowulf a clear Christological type.

But the great thing throughout this long poem is the view taken of God. We have grown far too comfortable with the name of our God. While our Lord did teach us to speak of Him as a Father, He insisted in the next breath that we hallow His name. But His name now comes off our lips far too readily, whether we curse or we bless. Breaking the third commandment comes easily to us, especially when we are looking at the words of that mantra-like song on the overhead projector.

But God is *Liffrea*—which means "Lord of life." When we look around us, it is astonishing that anything could live at all, still less live again. We have no account to give for it unless we acknowledge that our God is the living God, and God of all the living. Our fathers knew, living where they did, that the world around us is mostly indifferent and frequently hostile to the processes of life. We owe nothing to the created world around us; our debt for life is to the living Lord.

The living God is *wuldres Wealdend,* or "Ruler of glory." "Now the Lord of all life, Ruler of glory, blessed them with a prince, Beo" (11.16–17). Our contemporary theism is really a pathetic and sorry affair. We want an avuncular figure in the sky, someone to hand out celestial candies when we are feeling a little blue. But the true God is the Most High; He inhabits glory, and He is the sovereign Ruler of it. If invited to approach Him, if we actually understood what an invitation to approach unapproachable Light meant, we would cover our faces, completely abashed.

The Most High is *ece Drihten,* the "eternal Lord." "The Almighty drove those demons out." (1.108). In our earlier history, Thor and Odin had the power to frighten us—we are pitiful creatures who crawl on the ground, after all—but when all is said and done, we came through the kindness of the gospel to understand that they were mere creatures as well. Thunder is bigger than we are, but a creature still. Our gods lived with us, fellow wretches, on the outskirts of inexhaustible eternity. Only one is able to inhabit eternity, and He is the Almighty. The gospel came and ushered us into fellowship with that personal eternity through the Lord Christ.

The Almighty God is *sigora Sopcyning,* the "true King of victories." "No man could enter the tower, open hidden doors, unless the Lord of Victories, He who watches over men, Almighty God Himself, was moved to let him enter, and him alone" (11.3053–3057). Whether the victory is Grendel falling before Beowulf, or Satan crushed beneath the heel of Christ, God is the only One to bestow any victory. The psalmist asked the God of Israel to rise up and scatter His enemies; whenever the Power of His right hand is pleased to do so, those enemies are driven before Him like smoke in a gale. The Church today is a stranger to victories because we refuse to sing anthems to the king of all victories. We do not want a God of battles, we want sympathy for our surrenders. We need to be taught to sing as Alfred the Great taught his men before going into battle—"Jesu, defend us."

Before fighting Grendel, Beowulf declares that the results are in the hands of *witig God,* that is, "wise God." God's understanding, His wisdom, is infinite. We cannot see to the beginning of the end of it. We cannot define this infinitude by looking at a clear, night sky, but we may in this analogical manner get some *sense* of it. What does God not know? He is the only wise God. Hrothgar, the Danish king, also speaks of *wigtig Drihten,* the "wise Lord." He is the only wise Lord. What is this wisdom? *Who* is this wisdom?

Beowulf also acknowledges that the wise God is *halig Dryhten,* the "holy Lord." Our idea of holiness is greatly truncated today; we limit it in thousands of scrupling and schoolmarmish ways. We have lost any understanding of the *numinous.* We do not know what it would be like to walk through a grove of ancient trees sacred to the holy and terrible gods, and then be converted to the worship of One holier, and stranger, and mightier than these. We reject the shining of the ancient and numinous gods, not because we repudiate those gods as every Christian must, but because we have rejected the very idea of the numinous. We reject them, not because they are creatures, but because they remind us of the divine. This is not the holiness of Christianity, but rather the crass materialism of that great loser, modernity, and its ugly little sister, postmodernity.

Hrothgar says that Beowulf has overcome his enemy *þurh Dritnes miht,* which is to say, "through the power of the Lord." Beowulf had been given a tremendous power in his fighting grasp, but the glory for this strength and his subsequent victory is gladly attributed to the Lord of all power. Hrothgar also speaks of *Alwealdan,* the "Ruler of all." These early Christians, on the outlying borders of the medieval world, were no Deists, and they had fashioned no compromises with those who would rob God of His sovereignty. Hrothgar also lifts up *wuldres Hyrde,* the "Shepherd of glory."

Beowulf refers to the Lord as *Waldend fira,* the "Ruler of men," and *ecum Dryhtne,* the "eternal Lord," and *Wuldurcyninge,* the "King of glory."

> Who is this King of glory? The Lord strong and mighty, the Lord mighty in battle. Lift up your heads, O ye gates; even lift them up, ye everlasting doors; and the King of glory shall come in. Who is this King of glory? The Lord of hosts, he is the King of glory. (Ps. 24:8–10)

The way we think of God necessarily comes out in our speech; the way we refer to Him shows the condition of our hearts. One of the things which should immediately strike us as we read through this wonderful poem is the maturity which is most evident in the way God is reverenced when He is addressed and mentioned. This maturity stands in stark contrast to the breezy flippancy evident in the midst of most professing Christians today. In certain key respects, we corporately have clearly fallen from our first love. Compare this view with the idea of one modern evangelical writer, in which he argues that there are situations in which God "would like to answer [prayers] affirmatively but simply cannot." How sad.

Critical in the unfolding of *Beowulf* is the idea of *wyrd,* which, although it gives us our word "weird," primarily refers to "destiny" rather than simply to the strange or odd. The use of the word and concept in the poem is indebted to Boethius, and is therefore strongly linked to the Christian medievalism far to the south. The word refers to the unaccountably mysterious and uncanny destinies of men. We moderns have tidy little minds, and want a place for everything and everything in its place—we want the universe sorted out as though it were not any more complicated than the storage shelves in our garage. We have no room for the *wyrd,* for the idea that ineffable wisdom governs us in the most inscrutable ways. We, trapped in our thicket of time and chance, imagine there is nothing above or outside it. Because we do not know, because we do not see, it must not be there to be known or seen. The writer of Ecclesiastes knew better. "Then I beheld all the work of God, that a man cannot find out the work that is done under the sun: because though a man labor to seek it out, yet he shall not find it; yea further; though a wise man think to know it, yet shall he not be able to find it" (Eccl. 8:17). The author of *Beowulf* knew the same: "Then and now men must lie in their Maker's holy hands moved only as He wills: our hearts must seek out that will" (11.1057–1060). Centuries later Tennyson knew that if he could figure out an uprooted flower, he would know all things. The flower was therefore incomprehensible. The *wyrd* sets boundaries for us.

We who are now alive do not remember how to apprehend beauty and holiness of our God; we are so unlettered by modernity that we no longer ache to think of it. Our inability to comprehend such things pervades everything we do. Some hope that postmodernism will show the way out, but a postmodernist is nothing more than a modernist who has admitted his cultural illiteracy . . . which is not the same thing as reading. Christians by and large do not stand against this folly with a clear understanding of antithesis. Coming to worship the Lord in the "beauty of holiness" somehow gets translated into the "warmth of niceness." Almost entirely gone is the experience of being run through, pierced by the numinous. We acknowledge that some things are "pretty" or "nice," and desire to be dabbed by them. We say we call for the gods of glory and beauty but summon up the imbecilic and grinning demons of kitsch.

The answer is not *Beowulf*, but our tribes saw things then clearly which we do not see now. They saw their God. And consequently, we can say of this poem, as Lewis said of Tolkien's writing, "Here are beauties which pierce like swords or burn like cold iron; here is a book that will break your heart."

But how can we break our hearts until we have hearts to break? And how can we have hearts unless a *sovereign* God gives them to us?

CHAPTER 4

THE EMERGING DIVIDE

LOSING THE SERPENT . . . AND THE GREEKS

The final and eternal divide between the City of God and the City of Man will be determined by simple, personal embarrassment. On the one side of the chasm will be those who were too embarrassed to cling to Christ; on the other will be those who by grace were not embarrassed to be Christ's fools—"Let no man deceive himself. If any man among you seemeth to be wise in this world, let him become a fool, that he may be wise. For the wisdom of this world is foolishness with God" (1 Cor. 3:18–19).

The medieval attitude toward the truth of Christianity is a delight to behold. They lived it and breathed it. It was taken for granted by commoners and intellectual elites alike. Christianity was such comfortable, common furniture that its opponents looked clearly artificial. Even the unfaithful recognized that they lived in a world under the Lordship of Christ. These are all, of course, generalizations, but the obviousness of Christian truth permeates medieval thinking in the same way that sheepishness regarding Christian truth permeates modern Christian thinking. Medievals weren't frightened by their ideological opponents. After all, they had raced their ideological opponents and triumphed. The pagans longed to imitate Christian culture.

The final divide between the embarrassed and unembarrassed horrifies those moderns who take the Enlightenment seriously, but it should also horrify decent, clean-shaven modern Christians, because so many of us are instinctively embarrassed by the claims of the Christian view of reality. Though the Judgment will forever divide the embarrassed and the unembarrassed, the embarrassed do appear to be making up a large portion of professing Christians. Think for a moment about how many squabbles in the Church stem from not wanting to have moderns think we are unenlightened throwbacks . . . dare we say, medieval? Consider how agitated we get in our rush to assure our Enlightenment lords that scriptural faith endorses nothing so obviously embarrassing and unmodern and wicked as excommunication, the death penalty, patriarchalism, slavery, a young earth, and monarchy, or that Scripture condemns sodomy, public schools, recycling, or whatever else might make moderns shake their fingers at us.

But the important test question here isn't whether Christianity teaches egalitarianism or an old earth, *but what if it clearly didn't?* Would we be embarrassed then? What if Scripture really taught all those horrible things mocked so loudly by moderns—would we be ashamed? This is a wonderful personal test. Think of the most horrible moral or scientific accusation raised against the Christian faith and then ask, what if it's true? Would we be embarrassed to stand by Christ? Or could we thumb our noses at modern scowls? We are promised that idolatrous wisdom is less than false; it is foolishness. The very first commandment calls us to disdain all other loyalties and fear God alone. That sort of attitude makes up the radical Scriptural challenge, "Let God be true, but every man a liar" (Rom. 3:4). Every man? Could we stand firm if every scientific study and political expert denounced

Christian truth? Could you stand loyal and unembarrassed against laughter pouring forth from the president of N.O.W., Stephen J. Gould, and Calvin College? Evangelicals have tended to buckle their knees at much less. We don't know the great joy of swallowing the reductios from our opponents. Let them have their feeble idols; we have Christ.

Part of the medieval ability to appreciate the obviousness of Christianity was their maturing understanding of that ancient war between the seed of Eve and the seed of the Serpent, that deep antithesis between the friends and enemies of God. If we aren't in the midst of a war, then any talk of enemies and subversion sounds rather silly and paranoid. That is the modern Christian predicament. We agree with our contemporaries that we're all at peace, working toward the same pleasant neighborhood goals, when in fact we stand stupidly in the middle of a total war assuming we're at a banquet.

From the beginning, Scripture lays out the features of the antithesis between the friends and enemies of God. It was no accident. This war was divinely imposed—"And I will put enmity between thee and the woman, and between thy seed and her seed; it shall bruise thy head, and thou shalt bruise his heel" (Gen. 3:15). This war is not an option we can make disappear by visualizing world peace. Christ alone can usher in peace.

God held the knowledge of this battle up before the Old Covenant saints constantly. They knew the importance of genealogies, those much ignored passages. They knew the seed of the woman—Abel, Seth, Noah, Shem, Abraham, Isaac, Jacob, Moses, faithful Israel, David, the remnant of Judah—and their constant spiritual and physical struggle against the seed of the Serpent—Cain, the Nephilim, Ham, Nimrod, Ishmael, Esau, Egypt, Korah, the Canaanite, the

Northern tribes, Assyria, and Babylon. God's law itself pressed this antithesis into their day to day lives. The commandments not only called for loyalty to God, but even the details of the dietary laws were presented, not for health, but to remind the people of the antithesis:

> I am the Lord your God, which have separated you from other people. Ye shall therefore put difference between clean beasts and unclean, and between unclean fowls and clean. . . . And ye shall be holy unto me: for I the Lord am holy, and have severed you from other people, that ye should be mine. (Lev. 20:24–26)

We find the most striking teaching on the divine antithesis in the Psalms, the war songs of defeat and triumph. Modern Christians often have a very hard time thinking about some of the very real, flesh-and-blood enemies filling the Psalms. We want to deny the existence of enemies on earth, or we prefer to make them all just invisible shades, never rubbing up against them in physical life. But the antithesis is not so conveniently ignored, and the Psalms confront us powerfully.

The prophets confront us with the failure of God's people to hold fast the antithesis between light and darkness. Through the prophets, the Lord presses this failure forth primarily through the language of adultery: "How shall I pardon thee for this? Thy children have forsaken me, and sworn by them that are no gods: when I had fed them to the full, they then committed adultery, and assembled themselves by troops in the harlots' houses" (Jer. 5:7). Over and over again, the prophets condemn the people's sin as lusting after the other side of the divide, a yearning to imitate pagan ways.

The New Covenant recognizes Jesus as the Christ, the seed of Abraham, whom the Father promised "Sit thou at my right hand, until I make thine enemies thy footstool" (Ps. 110:1). In the New Testament this becomes,

> Then cometh the end, when he shall have delivered up the kingdom to God, even the Father; when he shall have put down all rule and all authority and power. For he must reign, till he hath put all enemies under his feet. (1 Cor. 15:24–25)

Christ never diminishes this call for antithesis. He contrasts the sharp divide in terms of light and darkness:

> And this is the condemnation, that light is come into the world, and men loved darkness rather than light, because their deeds were evil. For every one that doeth evil hateth the light, neither cometh to the light, lest his deeds should be reproved. (Jn. 3:19–20)

The Apostle Paul repeats the message of antithesis as,

> For what fellowship hath righteousness with unrighteousness? and what communion hath light with darkness? And what concord hath Christ with Belial? or what part hath he that believeth with an infidel? And what agreement hath the temple of God with idols? (2 Cor. 6:14–16)

The Apostle John states it as, "Love not the world, neither the things that are in the world. If any man love the world, the love of the Father is not in him" (1 Jn. 2:15). Similarly, James teaches, "Ye adulterers and adulteresses, know ye not that the friendship of the world is enmity with God? Whosoever therefore will be a friend of the world is the enemy of God" (Jas. 4:4).

This language of antithesis has always been part of the thinking of the Church. Every generation has to try to make sense of it. Augustine and Athanasius—West and East, certainly two of the founders and shapers of medievalism—stand out for powerful statements of the antithesis. Augustine does this most famously in his *City of God,* where he pits the seed of the serpent against the seed of the woman in terms of the City of Man and the City of God. He explains,

> I classify the human race into two branches: the one consists of those who live by human standards, the other of those who live according to God's will. I also call these two classes the two cities, speaking allegorically. By two cities I mean two societies of human beings, one of which is predestined to reign with God for all eternity, the other doomed to undergo eternal punishment with the Devil.[1]

Augustine goes on to describe the sinful instability of non-Christian culture. The City of Man ought to hold out no hope for Christians glancing around for other gods to imitate.

> The earthly city is generally divided against itself by litigation, by wars, by battles, by the pursuit of victories that bring death with them or at best are doomed to death. For if any section of that city has risen up in war against another part, it seeks to be victorious over other nations, though it is itself slave of base passions; and if, when victorious, it is exalted in its arrogance, that victory brings death in its train.[2]

The City of Man cannot continue; it has to fail. Cultural pessimism should be central for that culture.

Athanasius preceded Augustine in rejoicing over the demise of pagan culture.

> Since the Savior's advent in our midst, not only does idolatry no longer increase, but it is getting less and gradually ceasing to be. Similarly, not only does the wisdom of the

---

1. Augustine, *City of God* (New York: Penguin Books, 1987), Book XV.1, 595.
2. Ibid., XV.4, 599.

Greeks no longer make any progress, but that which used to be is disappearing. . . . On the other hand, while idolatry and everything else that opposes the faith of Christ is daily dwindling and weakening and falling, the Savior's teaching is increasing everywhere![3]

Athanasius's zeal against Greek philosophy continues as a strong medieval concern, though medieval theologians and philosophers often get bad press on this point. Medieval thinkers are portrayed as compromisers with paganism, synthesizers of Hellenism and Christianity. This they surely were at many points. But there is a large difference between being a synthesizer intentionally and being one accidentally. We are all synthesizers accidentally, even those who condemn medieval thinkers too quickly. But most medievals were far better, far more antithetical in their thinking, than we are. Christians who fault Aquinas for his Aristotelian categories are often those most entangled with Quine and Wittgenstein and Kuhn. A thousand years from now better Christians will see our blind compromises with unbelief (if our century is remembered at all—which I doubt). And they'll be right. It would be nice to escape modernism wholly, but no one can see his own blind spots.

We need to extend some courtesy to the medievals, for they did much better than we do in understanding the divide between Christian and non-Christian thought. In the high and late medieval battle (and a battle it surely was) between Christianity and Greek thought, the Christians were unashamedly and self-consciously using Christian metaphysics to drive out Hellenism. The best part of the story is that it was Christian philosophers who pulled off one of the most

3. Athanasius, *On the Incarnation* (Crestwood: St. Vladimir's Seminary Press, 1993), 91–92, §55.

wonderful and unique philosophical coups in the history of philosophy. No other group has played such a pivotal part in philosophy. The history of philosophy forms a watershed at the high and late middle ages, and the division between these two periods is all the doing of Christians.

Plato was the chief philosophical enemy of medieval Christian philosophers, especially Thomas Aquinas. Plato was viewed as a respectable enemy but an enemy of the faith nonetheless, whose chief deficiency was his denigration of matter. Christian philosophers rightly rejoiced in matter and body and skin and toes, since God the Son Himself took them on, and the Triune God had declared the material world good. This produced a head-on collision between Christianity and Hellenism, and this was the first time these two worldviews had really met at this level. Aquinas's mistake was to dip into Aristotle's toolbox for help, since Aristotle appeared much more friendly to matter. But other Christian philosophers recognized Aristotle's failures as well as Plato's. Those who rejected both Plato and Aristotle would later be lumped together and tagged "nominalists." What motivated the more consistently Christian thinkers of this time was a second failing of Hellenism: *it ruled out knowledge of particular things,* such as this toad, this fingernail, this God. Aristotelian knowledge, just like Platonic, was obsessed with unity and could never truly get to knowledge of individual things, as much as Aquinas and Scotus would try to tweak it.

This hostility to knowledge of individuals was simply incompatible with a Christian worldview. After all, God knows us, and we know God, and humans must know each other, and we're all individuals. All of Hellenism must go, said the more consistent Christian philosophers. If that discussion would have continued, we would have found a more balanced Trinitarianism between the twin extremes of Hellenism and nominalism. But it didn't. Various social pressures took over, and the distinctively Christian concern with knowing concrete things was secularized into an exaggerated nominalistic concern with particulars, and the myths of modernity undid the wonderful medieval Christian triumph.

The people of God often take so long to understand the particular shape of the divine antithesis within a specific culture. Finding the divide is often a difficult process, but finding it is part of Christian sanctification. Sometimes Christians have drawn the line in the wrong place entirely (prohibitionist fundamentalism comes to mind). Sometimes Christians think that everything in life is the dividing line, thus turning every great and trivial issue into a fight to the death (perfectionistic presbyterianism comes to mind). Many Christians, however, fail to draw any line at all, synthesizing their thought with anything pagan that hops along. We must find the line where God draws it and that often takes sober, mature effort. Sometimes it's easy, much to the chagrin of those who are always wrestling with issues and never making a decision. But we don't have to do this anew every generation. We stand on the shoulders of the early and medieval Christian fathers who faced many of the same temptations as we do. Now they didn't always get it right, but only nearsightedness would say that we have it right now. If we want future Christians to be merciful to our mistakes—keeping the best, tossing out our blind spots—then we need to offer the same mercy to our forefathers in the faith. Protestants have been too quick to write off medieval thinking as hopelessly compromised.

The Enlightenment idol is science, an idol which has gripped and throttled orthodoxy for two centuries. But it has done so in a most curious way, surely not the most rational manner. Science sells. Neil Postman likes to tell stories about how he can get people to warm up to absurd ideas just by suggesting that some large university has produced research on the topic. Attaching "produced at Berkeley, Harvard, MIT" to a ridiculous argument immediately makes it cogent to many. That's part of life, but let's not pretend that it's rationality.

The odd thing is that science has a rather ridiculous track record to serve as such a powerful veto-house of truth. If we think in terms of centuries and millennia, few other disciplines turn inside-out so flippantly and quickly as the natural sciences. Nothing can take the puff out of the scientific chest more than a study of its history. Perhaps that's why it's so rare to find science departments requiring courses in the history of science. The history of science provides great strength to the inductive inference that, at any point in its history, *that day's science will almost certainly be deemed false, if not laughable, within a century (often in much less time).* As the saying goes, if you marry the science of today, you will be a widow tomorrow.

If the history of science were a single person, we certainly wouldn't let that person drive heavy machinery or carry sharp objects. Nonetheless, he could serve some useful functions. And he might do some better than others. But to set him up as the premier standard and priest of rationality is a bit too much to ask. We need to evaluate science with a more long-term, medieval view.

The world would look radically different if we were to judge it in medieval perspective, in terms of millennia. Good science requires multiple tests over decades. We can only improve science, then, by extending the testing time. Modern science is far too hasty, calling claims "knowledge" which are only a decade old. A claim that is only a decade old shouldn't even count as a belief, let alone knowledge. Given

science's fickleness, a more medieval mind would call a claim
that has lasted only one hundred years the "beginning of an
assertion." Scientific claims that stand up for five hundred
years we may begrudgingly call "weak conjectures," but certainly not a well-founded belief. And then perhaps, those
rare claims that stand firm well beyond a millennium or two
at the very least, we can start to call strong beliefs. In such a
more patient, more mature, more medieval, more scientific
perspective, scientific claims can flit about week by week as
much as they like without trashing the permanent things.

But moderns will certainly balk at such long term constraints, a balk that reveals their hatred of knowledge and
love for grants and press releases. Our modern, hasty science
is so much like the ancient Athens of Paul's time, "given over
to idols," spending "their time in nothing else but either to
tell or to hear some new thing" (Acts 17:21). We are in love
with the ugliness of novelty. Yet at the heart of Christian
thinking about antithesis is a skepticism of novelty—"be
no more children, tossed to and fro, and carried about with
every wind of doctrine, by the sleight of men, and cunning
craftiness, whereby they lie in wait to deceive" (Eph. 4:14).
In trying to understand the ancient antithesis in our day,
we need to raise the banner of a Christian skepticism which
doubts all novelty and pagan claims for at least a millennium.
If we were to do just that, we would go far in our maturity,
far in faithfulness to the call, "Let God be true, though every man a liar." Then, by the grace of God, we could then
bow on the last day at the feet of Christ on the side of the
unembarrassed.

CHAPTER 5

WHERE RIGHTEOUSNESS AND MERCY KISS

DEEP THANKS FOR THE PROTESTANT HEART

"But," said Peace, "I can prove that their pain must come to an end, and suffering is bound to turn to happiness in the end. For if they had never known any suffering, they could never know happiness. No man can grasp what pleasure is who has never suffered, or understand hunger who has never been without food. I am sure that if there were no night, no one would know for certain the meaning of day! . . . For until we meet with Scarcity no one knows what it is to have enough. And so God of His goodness placed the first man, Adam, in a state of contentment and perfect happiness, and then allowed him to sin and experience sorrow, so that he might learn for himself what real happiness was."

—Langland, *Piers Plowman*

The high and late middle ages meditated deeply on the tension between God's justice and mercy. How could a perfectly holy God forgive? The blossom of that wonderful meditation developed into the excited joy of the Reformation's understanding of justification—that holy and merciful exchange of our guilt and punishment for Christ's righteousness—justice and mercy reconciled. The beginnings of that debate started within that crucial medieval struggle between Hellenism and Christian Hebraism. Rome kept to the Greek side of that divide, embracing its Aristotelian schema of created, substantive graces and incomplete righteousness, while the road to the Reformation embraced the biblical, Hebraic notions of covenants, imputation, representation, and perfect righteousness. But that is the climax of the story. The drama up to that point reveals an engaging medieval tale.

"I am sure that if there were no night, no one would know for certain the meaning of day!" reads Langland's medieval poem above. Consider how many bleak twilights and black nights shrouded God's people before the advent of His Son—our kinsman Redeemer. It's hard to imagine a darker time in the history of faith than the Old Covenant exile from Jerusalem. Israel had been taken to the heights of joy and triumph. God had promised His people unspeakable prosperity, all secured in the glorious promises of an eternal throne under kingly shepherds of David's seed. But Israel's world started to splinter and dissolve before their very eyes. Violence shattered the faithful, and the rebellious seemed to triumph. Elijah even thought he was alone. Had God lied to David? What had become of the promise? Had God ceased to be God? Jeremiah himself lamented,

> How doth the city sit solitary, that was full of people! How is she become as a widow! . . . She weepeth sore in the night, and her tears are on her cheeks: among all her lovers she hath none to comfort her: all her friends have dealt treacherously with her, they are become her enemies. . . . The ways of Zion do mourn, because none come to the solemn feasts: all her gates are desolate: her priests sigh, her virgins are afflicted, and she is in bitterness. Her adversaries are the chief, her enemies prosper; for the Lord hath afflicted her for the multitude of her transgressions. (Lam. 1:1–5)

So much had been thrown away, so much squandered. Loneliness and terror and hopelessness consumed everything.

Into the midst of such darkness an excruciating theological tension bore down upon their thinking—justice against mercy, righteousness against peace. Even in the midst of Israel's steaming cauldron, the Lord promised reconciliation. He told the faithful of a wonderful future of mercy for them, yet at the same time He promised that every sin would be punished to the fullest extent of His holiness. What joy! What horror! The haunting medieval hymn chants this despair to us every year, *"Veni, veni Emmanuel / Captivum solve Israel, / Qui gemit in exilio, / Privatus Dei filio"*—or as we now sing, "O come, O come, Emmanuel, / And ransom captive Israel, / That mourns in lonely exile here, / Until the Son of God appear."

Langland's *Piers Plowman* devotes its culminating chapter to a moving debate between the four daughters of God—Peace, Righteousness, Truth, and Mercy as they quarrel over the momentous display of the crucifixion. Peace is dressed in the clothes of celebration heading off to "welcome all the lost souls, whom I have not seen for many a long day now, because of the darkness of sin." Righteousness stops her joy short with, "Have you gone off your head? or had you too much to drink? Do you really suppose that this light [of the resurrection] can unlock hell, and save the souls of men? Don't you believe it! God Himself pronounced this doom in the beginning, that Adam and Eve and all their seed should surely die, and after death live in torment. . . . I am Righteousness, and I tell you this for certain: that their suffering will never cease, and no prayer can ever help them."

Their quarrel continues until Christ, "the Son of the King of Heaven," unbars the gates and conquers Lucifer. He explains to all how He reconciles holiness and forgiveness in

His sacrifice—"I can grant them mercy without offending justice, and all my words remain true." Then joy bursts forth from angels harp and song, and Peace sings, "No weather is warmer than after the blackest clouds." Truth relents and confesses, "'You are in the right, Mercy. Let us make our peace together, and seal it with a kiss.' 'And nobody shall know that we ever quarrelled,' said Peace, 'for nothing is impossible with Almighty God.'" And then we read those wonderful lines, "Mercy and Truth are met together: Righteousness and Peace have kissed each other."

The reconciliation of righteousness and mercy is the main theme which drove forward the medieval heart of the Protestant Reformation. Of the early Puritans, C. S. Lewis remarked, "Whatever they were, they were not sour, gloomy, or severe; Nor did their enemies bring any such charge against them. . . . For [Thomas] More, a Protestant was one 'Dronke of the new must, of lewd lightnes of minde and vayne gladnessese of harte'. . . . Protestantism was not too grim but too glad to be true."[1] *Too glad to be true*—what a wonderful summary of the fruit of the Protestant doctrine of justification!

How things have changed. In our day, evangelicals almost yearn to be described as "sour, gloomy, and severe," as we grovel in our self-centered pietism and political campaigns for external morality. What a different world we would live in if *Christians* were characterized, not as those calling for Federal prohibitions on this and that, but for the right to celebrate? What if we were known *by our enemies,* not for our shallow sentimentalism and indifference to beauty, but as that community most exuberantly living life to the fullest,

---

1. C. S. Lewis, *English Literature in the Sixteenth Century* (Oxford: Clarendon Press, 1954), 33–34.

full of eating, drinking, and merriment (Eccl. 8:15)? Perhaps then we could be slandered like our Lord for being gluttons, winebibbers, and friends of sinners (Mt. 11:19). The exuberance characteristic of the early Protestants wasn't the thin fanaticism of a Finney revival, but the life-changing shock of unexpected liberation, the joy of justification in Christ.

Consider how Rome's story of justification fails to resolve the divine drama between justice and mercy. Before medieval high scholasticism, the fathers of the Church viewed justification in more personal terms as an encounter between man and God. Some even spoke in terms of imputation of righteousness, but their calling was to clarify Christology and the Trinity, which they did wonderfully. In the providence of God, the medievals, beginning with Anselm, had the theological duty of clarifying the doctrine of justification.

As one contemporary Thomist informs us, the thirteenth century was "the first decisive philosophical encounter between Hellenism and Christianity." There we find Christian thinkers seeking diligently to discern the antithesis between Platonic-Aristotelian thinking from Christian Hebraic thinking. As heroic as Thomas Aquinas was in many antithetical respects, in the end, he remained within an Aristotelian mold in understanding justification. He and many other medieval thinkers constructed and refined the novel Roman schema of *created grace* as the intermediary between God and man in justification. They argued that justification involves an Aristotelian ontological change in man, a real, substantive grace attaching to the soul in order for man to be justified before God. This substantive grace—the created habit of grace or charity—became a necessary element of justification. This Greek schema became cemented into the Roman tradition in various councils, especially Trent. Aristotle can still be heard in statements from such contemporary Roman

Catholic thinkers as Frank Sheed: "When we come to die there is only one question that matters—have we sanctifying grace in our souls?"

In the broadest strokes, the Roman-Aristotelian solution to the tension between God's righteousness and mercy is twofold: first, Rome affirms that Christ paid a commercial sacrifice but denies that Christ bore the guilt of our sins; second, Christ's commercial payment opens the door for us to receive created grace, specifically sanctifying grace into our souls through the sacraments of the Church. On this scheme, Christ satisfies God's righteousness via a commercial substitute (Christ pays our fine) and makes us righteous by filling us with sanctifying grace. If we lose sanctifying grace through mortal sin or muddy it with venial sin, we can still recover it via more sacraments. At death, if we lack sufficient sanctifying grace or have besmirched it, then we can be perfected through the fires of purgatory.

But notice how this Aristotelianism fails to resolve the divine drama. Instead of reconciling God's perfect holiness with His mercy, Rome has God lower His standards of righteousness; He no longer demands perfection. God can be at peace with persons (even before purgatory) who merely have enough sanctifying grace in their souls, muddied as it might be by venial sin. Mercy mugs justice. Even worse, Rome embraces a legal atrocity in its sacrifice of Christ. By denying that Christ bears the guilt of our sins, it wants us to believe that God kills His Son though He bears no guilt. Then the Father slays the innocent. Here justice is exiled. For the Roman story, then, God not only suspends His holiness, He violates His own just command—"slay thou not the innocent and righteous" (Exod. 23:7). Instead of having righteousness and mercy kiss in elegant drama, Rome tells a cheap Aristotelian horror story.

But the Roman novelty of Aristotelian graces was not the only medieval story gaining prominence. At the same time, other Christian medievalists were more consistently casting off both Plato and Aristotle, while reviving the Hebraic concepts of covenants. In various degrees, they removed all ground for the metaphysics of created graces and moved toward a more personal view of justification. These Augustinian thinkers sought to preserve the liberty of God, freeing Him from Greek constraints, and they found better refuge in Hebraic categories. This more distinctively Christian tradition of justification laid the groundwork for the Reformers to speak more clearly of covenants, representation, imputation, and perfect righteousness:

> Those whom God effectually calleth he also freely justifieth; not by infusing righteousness into them, but by pardoning their sins, and by accounting and accepting their persons as righteous . . . by imputing the obedience and satisfaction of Christ unto them, they receiving and resting on him and his righteousness by faith . . . Christ, by His obedience and death, did fully discharge the debt of all those that are thus justified, and did make a proper, real, and full satisfaction to his Father's justice in their behalf . . . that both the exact justice and rich grace of God might be glorified in the justification of sinners.[2]

Notice how seriously the Protestants take the drama between justice and mercy. It is crucial that they kiss. They do not diminish God's holiness or resort to legal atrocities or fictions. Covenantal representation is very real, though it doesn't fit into an Aristotelian framework. The Greek view of reality was always narrower than Scripture's. And so the Protestant view does justice to the soul-wrenching, dramatic tension announced in the Old Covenant. How can a perfectly

2. *Westminster Confession of Faith*, XI.1, 3.

holy God forgive a sinful people? He does so by the reality of covenantal representation. He pours out His just wrath on His Son, the covenantal representative, the second Adam, and He shows grace, mercy, and peace to His people who have had Christ's perfect righteousness imputed to them. Righteousness and Mercy kiss in the most unexpected, unbelievable manner. Too glad to be true!

In the Reformers, we find the triumph of the medieval Hebraism, which began hundreds of years prior to the culmination of the medieval battle against Greek synthesis. Rome, on the other hand, turns out to be a sterile regress, a regress locked "irreformably" in the Greek categories that the early and medieval fathers fought so nobly to escape.

The early and medieval fathers provide us with wonderful glimpses of the culmination of the very medieval doctrine of the Reformers. The doctrine wasn't always perfectly clear, just as in the doctrine of the Trinity, but it was always there. Listen to the music of justification from one Mathetes, in his epistle to Diognetus in the second century:

> He Himself took on Him the burden of our iniquities, He gave His own Son as a ransom for us, the holy One for transgressors, the blameless One for the wicked, the righteous One for the unrighteous, the incorruptible One for the corruptible, the immortal One for them that are mortal. For what other thing was capable of covering our sins than His righteousness? By what other one was it possible that we, the wicked and ungodly, could be justified, than by the only Son of God? O sweet exchange! O unsearchable operation! O benefits surpassing all expectation! that the wickedness of many should be hid in a single righteous One, and that the righteousness of One should justify many transgressors.[3]

3. "Epistle of Mathetes to Diognetes," in *The Ante-Nicene Fathers*, vol. 1, eds. A. Roberts and J. Donaldson (Peabody: Hendrickson Publ., Inc., 1994), 25.

At the other end of the millennium we can hear the same song of justification from Anselm, that great father who affected so much of the entire medieval debate:

> When a brother seems to be in his death struggle, it is godly and advisable to exercise him through a prelate or other priest with written questions and exhortations. He may be asked in the first place: "Brother, are you glad that you will die in the faith?" Let him answer: "Yes." "Do you confess that you did not live as well as you should have?" "I confess." "Are you sorry for this?" "Yes." "Are you willing to better yourself if you should have further time to live?" "Yes." "Do you believe that the Lord Jesus Christ, the Son of God, has died for you?" "Yes." "Do you believe that you cannot be saved except through His death?" "Yes." "Do you heartily thank Him for this?" "Yes." "Therefore always give thanks to Him while your soul is in you, and on this death alone place your whole confidence. Commit yourself wholly to this death, with this death cover yourself wholly, and wrap yourself in it completely. And if the Lord should want to judge you, say: 'Lord, I place the death of our Lord Jesus Christ between me and Thee and Thy judgment; I will not contend with Thee in any other way.' If He says that you have merited damnation, say: 'I place the death of our Lord Jesus Christ between myself and my evil deserts, and the merits of His most worthy passion I bring in place of the merit which I should have had, and, alas, do not have.'" He shall say further: "The death of our Lord Jesus Christ I set between me and Thy wrath." Then he shall say three times: "Into Thy hands, Lord, I commend my spirit." And the gathering of those standing about him shall respond: "Into Thy hands, Lord, we commend his spirit." And he shall die safely and shall not see death eternally.[4]

4. Cited in John Owen, *Justification* (Edinburgh: Banner of Truth Trust, 1971 [1677]), 16–17. A Latin and a fifteenth-century English version of this death-bed confession can be found in R. W. Southern and F. S.

Anselm gives us medievalism and "Protestantism" in one wonderful summary. Too glad to be true.

Schmitt, *Memorials of St. Anselm* (London: Oxford University Press, 1969), 353–354.

CHAPTER 6

THE FONT OF LAUGHTER

WHERE JOY AND GRATITUDE OVERFLOW

O what their joy and their glory must be,
Those endless sabbaths the blessed ones see!

—Peter Abelard

Truth is, of course, rigid and unyielding. But some truths are more obviously rigid, and when they are embraced falsely, those who misconstrue them are made rigid as well. This is why the touchstone for the right kind of doctrine must be the right kind of joy and laughter. Jesus taught us that doctrine or teaching is to be evaluated by the kind of fruit it produces. If one wants to know if it is the right kind of tree, then he must check to see if it bears the right kind of fruit. Laughter and gladness are where joy, contentment, and gratitude overflow. But in an odd turn, these things proceed from an understanding of the truths of man's utter depravity and the salvation of the Lord.

Certainly we are warned against many kinds of counterfeit laughter. The laughter of empty fools is empty itself; God takes no pleasure in the cackling of fools. "It is better to hear the rebuke of the wise, than for a man to hear the song of fools. For as the crackling of thorns under a pot, so is the laughter of the fool: this also is vanity" (Eccl. 7:5–6).

So the laughter we are seeking is not the manic chortling of the nightclub comedians. We are not looking to the laugh track, that great comedic cattle prod, as some sort of moral compass for the desperate.

But how could a rejection of the counterfeit be taken as hatred of the real? We do not turn away from a self-willed laughter into a self-willed gloom. We are creatures of the Lord; everything we are and do is in His hands. Because He will bring this world to salvation through the resurrection of His Son, we must therefore glory in what He has done. The apostle tells us that Jesus went to the cross because of *the joy that was set before Him.* Christ endured the cross while looking toward the joy on the other side of His passion. And when Christ rose from the dead, His followers were overwhelmed by their own joy. They were frankly undone by it. Initially this joy was an emotionally stupefying joy—a drastic relief from the tumultuous events of the previous week. Luke even tells us that they *did not believe for joy.* Such joy was a very natural response, considering. When the Lord went up into heaven, we are told the disciples returned to Jerusalem with great joy. But this sense of emotional relief cannot be sustained for thousands of years, and hence the point of the scriptural commands to rejoice. We must have a standing and disciplined joy. This discipline of joy and Christian laughter is essential, and it must come from *comprehending* the culmination of God's kindness to us in the resurrection. This has always been the case.

After all, in the resurrection we have been released from our iniquities. "Unto you first God, having raised up his Son Jesus, sent him to bless you, in turning away every one of you *from his iniquities*" (Acts 3:26). In our acceptance of the apostolic witness to the resurrection, God visits us in power, and brings the grace of joy and laughter. "And with *great power* gave the apostles witness of the resurrection of the Lord Jesus: and *great grace* was upon them all" (Acts 4:33). In the resurrection of Christ, we have come into a hope which lives and breathes. "Blessed be the God and Father of our Lord Jesus Christ, which according to his abundant mercy hath begotten us again *unto a lively hope* by the resurrection of Jesus Christ from the dead" (1 Pet. 1:3).

We see the first inklings of the gospel's trajectory in the faith of Abraham, the father of all who share his faith. Many events in his life point to the salvation we have now been given in Christ. Every faithful believer recalls how he took his only son Isaac to the region of Moriah, to sacrifice him there. Moriah was the same area where, centuries later, the Lord Jesus died—*God's* only Son. When Isaac was first promised to Abraham, consider his response: "Then Abraham fell upon his face, and *laughed,* and said in his heart, 'Shall a child be born unto him that is a hundred years old? and shall Sarah, that is ninety years old, bear?'" (Gen. 17:17). And in the next chapter, Sarah does the same thing (Gen. 18:13–15). But for the laughter of disbelief God substitutes another kind. When the child comes, God insists he be named Isaac, which means *he laughs* (Gen. 17:19). The child of promise is a promise of laughter.

When we come to the New Testament, we see the believers there looking back at God's great promises.

> For David speaketh concerning him, "I foresaw the Lord always before my face; for he is on my right hand, that I should not be moved: Therefore did my heart *rejoice,* and my tongue was *glad;* moreover also my flesh shall rest in hope: Because thou wilt not leave my soul in hell, neither wilt thou suffer thine Holy One to see corruption. Thou hast made known to me the ways of life; *thou shalt make me full of joy with thy countenance.*" (Acts 2:25–28)

The quoted prophecy from Psalm 16 goes on to make it even more plain—at God's right hand are resurrection pleasures into eternity. "Thou wilt show me the path of life: in thy presence is *fulness of joy;* at thy right hand there are *pleasures for evermore*" (Ps. 16:11).

As we learn what it means to think as Christians, to think as though life really did conquer death, we will learn to join our voices to those who were delivered from an earlier exile. We will join them in their dream.

> When the Lord turned again the captivity of Zion, we were like them that dream. *Then was our mouth filled with laughter, and our tongue with singing:* then said they among the heathen, 'The Lord hath done great things for them.' The Lord hath done great things for us; whereof *we are glad.* Turn again our captivity, O Lord, as the streams in the south. They that sow in tears shall reap *in joy.* He that goeth forth and weepeth, bearing precious seed, *shall doubtless come again with rejoicing,* bringing his sheaves with him. (Ps. 126:1–6)

"Blessed are ye that weep now: for ye shall *laugh*" (Lk. 6:21b). The truth of the gospel leads inexorably to laughter. Those who want to glower as they cling to truth want something that can never be. Whatever it is they have in their hands, it must not be the truth, unless it is perhaps just a fragment of it. The dour Calvinist, the cranky sabbatarian, and the pious self-loather are all textbook head cases. We see them in Scripture, we see them in our literature, and sometimes we see them out on their front porch on sabbath afternoons, glaring at the bicyclists. Are they speaking the truth? Well . . . are they laughing for joy?

Whenever truth is presented to us, we have to recognize the various devices we have for avoiding it. The libertine is not hard to understand. Any given truth may be overtly rejected in the flesh. But we too often forget that it may also be accepted and praised in the flesh. Thus the pharisaical mind is inoculated to truth—he has received just enough of the truth to keep him from getting a case of the real thing.

And this is how certain truths are brought into disrepute. We think a good deal of misery in the world must have been caused by the severities of Christianity, particularly the truths concerning predestination and the realities of our own depravity and sinfulness. The image draws a great deal of its force from the caricatures that we tend to manufacture in our minds. Is it not obvious that anyone who believes in human depravity must be angry and dour? But it really draws no force at all from the logic inherent in these truths, and all the false applications made from them are really *non sequiturs* of the first order of magnitude.

It is easy for modern Christians to think of Luther, Calvin, and Zwingli standing around a cauldron at the beginning of some reformational *Macbeth,* coming up with the doctrines of predestination and depravity. The lightning flashes, the murky brew belches a loathsome smell, and one can readily tell by the pricking of his thumbs that it is time to try to find another church. These people here believe harsh and horrible things. But rightly understood, to use Tyndale's phrase, the doctrine is really the soft rain of grace after the thunder of the law. In a parched land, the goodness of God's salvation falls wonderfully, and predestination is simply a glorious redemption given from the hand of the Lord. It is not surprising that the effect it has on men who understand it is that of a redeemed gut chuckle. As C. S. Lewis pointed out, for men like Tyndale, "amid all [his] severities there is something like laughter, that laughter which he speaks of as coming 'from the low bottom of the heart.'"[1] This is a laughter which comes naturally—the fruit of the grace of God is joy and gladness and laughter.

1. Lewis, *English Literature,* 192.

But what of the teaching that man is hopelessly depraved, that he is nothing else by nature than hell-fodder crawling around? Why such a disparaging view? Is this not a low view of man? But the dominical saying should bring us up short. The one who is forgiven much loves much. The one who does not love much, the one who placidly continues a decent middle-class religious existence can be safely dismissed as one who did not understand the words of his catechism. The Pharisee can walk solemnly through his synagogue a thousand times, and each time be filthier than the last time. But the whore who has been underneath a thousand men can laugh with joy because her sins are *forgiven*. Such women were in Christ's entourage. How can a whore find the God of her salvation? And if she does, what is that like? "Behold, God is my salvation; I will trust, and not be afraid: for the Lord Jehovah is my strength and my song; he also is become my salvation. Therefore *with joy* shall ye draw water out of the wells of salvation" (Is. 12:2–3). A woman of loose morals once stood with our Lord next to a well in Samaria, and He offered her some observations on this same subject.

A man who has been saved from death will not be made gloomy by realizing how great the danger was. If a man is saved from falling over a cliff, we will not make him cantankerous by informing him that the cliff was a thousand feet high. His relief and joy and gladness would be all the greater. If he were to fly into a rage over it, we would have grounds for assuming that he did not really understand the good news.

False assumptions about spirituality have crept into our thinking in countless ways. "The spiritual ethereal realm is good, and the earthly material realm is gross and worldly. The pious man, the man who is heavenly-minded, is someone who knows heavenly raptures, utterly unlike what we can know here and now. It is so unlike our customary experience that is usually manifested here by a dour and gloomy countenance."

If anyone objects to the obvious problems in this line of reasoning, he may be reminded that God's thoughts are not our thoughts, and His ways are not our ways. Heavenly joy must be earthly gloom, and vice versa. The first shall be last, and the joyful shall scowl.

But this is clearly wrong. In this futile world, in this world where vanity reigns, we can know that the grace of God has burst through to us by one indication only: "Go thy way, eat thy bread with joy, and drink thy wine with a merry heart; for God now accepteth thy works" (Eccl. 9:7). A man who stands in his justification is a man who has been enabled to really enjoy the bread on his table and the wine in his glass. But a man who is left to his own devices is a man who can eat and drink, yet cannot *taste*.

> For God giveth to a man that is good in his sight, wisdom, and knowledge, and joy: but to the sinner he giveth travail, to gather and to heap up, that he may give to him that is good before God. This also is vanity and vexation of spirit. (Eccl. 2:26)

The godly are characterized by gladness. The doctrines of godliness are the doctrines of gladness. If it does not come at the last to gladness, then to hell with it. When the work of God is good and deep, then those who are redeemed from their depravity are happy to sing and talk about it. "And the ransomed of the Lord shall return, and come to Zion with songs and everlasting joy upon their heads: they shall obtain joy and gladness, and sorrow and sighing shall flee away" (Is. 35:10). When they really understand that God foreordained their wonderful salvation before the foundations of the world, they break into another song. Too often Christians debate the fact of predestination in such a way that both sides forget what a wonderful doctrine it would be if it were true. "Break forth into joy, sing together, ye waste places of Jerusalem: for the Lord hath comforted his people, he hath redeemed Jerusalem" (Is. 52:9). The real stakes in the real debate are joy and laughter.

But the friends of these truths sometimes forget these ramifications as often as the adversaries of these truths do. We have many Christians who embrace the truth about pre-destination simply because it still makes other people mad, and it provides them with the opportunity to move on to other issues which make other people mad. Soon the regula-tive principle is wound tight around their axle; they are so full of scruples that they are standing in the slop of the over-flow. They insist, for example, that we now have a bounden duty to sing the psalms; we must sing the psalms; gotta sing psalms; in sin if you don't sing psalms. In attitude, this is the antithesis of joy. "Is any among you afflicted? let him pray. Is any *merry?* let him sing psalms" (Jas. 5:13).

When the Lord musters His accusations against the peo-ple of the Lord, He charges them for missing this. "Because thou servedst not the Lord thy God with joyfulness, and with gladness of heart, for the abundance of all things" (Deut. 28:47). As the Lord sums up all the curses He would bring upon the people for disobedience, He tells them in effect that they will be expelled from the land for not having had a good enough time there. The godly have learned that idolatry is a sin; they have not yet fully learned that idolatry is a drag.

> For great is the Lord, and greatly to be praised: he also is to be feared above all gods. For all the gods of the people are idols: but the Lord made the heavens. Glory and honour are in *his* presence; strength and gladness are in *his* place. (1 Chr. 16:25–27)

Glory and honor, strength and gladness.

When we learn our depravity in Adam, and we see in our lives how that depravity is manifested, and we see how

God determined to send His Son to be a great deliverer for His people, and we see how that predetermined plan was implemented in the death and resurrection of our Lord Jesus, how can we consistently respond with anything *but* the laughter of joy? This deliverance, this salvation of ours, is the greatest deliverance ever accomplished in the history of our race. Why do we act as though nothing happened? Even a temporal deliverance brings about some recognition of the fact. "The Jews had light, and gladness, and joy, and honour. And in every province, and in every city, whithersoever the king's commandment and his decree came, the Jews had joy and gladness, a feast and a good day" (Est. 8:16–17).

We are sadly mistaken and think that fussiness is holiness. We think the Lord's Day is for fasting when it is a feast. We think that psalms were given to mortify the flesh when they were in fact given for the overflow of the spirit. We think that predestination is a vast and impersonal machine grinding our bones into flour, when it's nothing other than our loving Father involved in everything we say and do. In our poverty-stricken doctrine, our salvation was God's little afterthought, and besides, we were not that bad to begin with, and so we have been forgiven little, and have received little. Not surprisingly, we love little and laugh even less.

The way out is repentance—not a worldly sorrow that leads to death, but a godly sorrow that leads to repentance without regret. In another time of reformation, the people had to be reminded of the same thing. A return to holiness is always a return to joy and laughter. "Then he said unto them, Go your way, eat the fat, and drink the sweet, and send portions unto them for whom nothing is prepared: for *this day is holy* unto our Lord: *neither be ye sorry; for the joy of the Lord is your strength*" (Neh. 8:10).

The Church today is filled with those who do not want the liberating effects of the gospel to get loose. They want some kennel-fed gospel, something they can control. They do not believe such expectations to be realistic. "There be many that say, 'Who will show us any good?' Lord, lift thou up the light of thy countenance upon us. Thou hast put gladness in my heart, more than in the time that their corn and their wine increased" (Ps. 4:6–7). These promises of God are seen and understood by faith.

A Christianity which understands the covenants of promise is a faith that will be filled to overflowing with joy and laughter, music and dancing.

> For the Lord shall comfort Zion: he will comfort all her waste places; and he will make her wilderness like Eden, and her desert like the garden of the Lord; joy and gladness shall be found therein, thanksgiving, and the voice of melody. (Is. 51:3)

If these things are so, it appears that the Church today has grossly misunderstood the demeanor which the Bible describes. Either we ignore the tenor of Scripture and gravitate to those selected doctrines which we can assemble into systematic theologies as though they were tinker toys, or we look at such passages and think we fulfill them by aping the laughter of the world, a laughter as hollow as a jug.

The Word rebukes our sidelong glances at the world. Not that kind of laughter. The Word rebukes our choreographed repentance. Not that sanctimonious smarminess. "Whom having not seen, ye love; in whom, though now ye see him not, yet believing, ye rejoice with *joy unspeakable* and *full of glory:* Receiving the end of your faith, even *the salvation of your souls*" (1 Pet. 1:8–9). A man who looks at this and does not laugh for joy does not understand. He has not really confessed his Christianity; he has not spoken the creed in truth. He has a heart of stone, and a head to match.

CHAPTER 7

WORSHIPING WITH BODY

FEASTING ON FOOD AND MARRIAGE

We so often lead lives forgetful of the fact that our God is very shocking. Amidst all our fragile piety and devouring busyness, we have a Lord who steps in and *commands* us such things as,

> Thou shalt bestow that money for whatsoever thy soul lusteth after, for oxen, or for sheep, or for wine, or for strong drink, or for whatsoever thy soul desireth: and thou shalt eat there before the Lord thy God, and thou shalt rejoice, thou, and thine household. (Deut. 14:26)

Such unthriftiness. Such waste. Such gluttony. Such winebibbing. Such is a command of our holy God.

For some reason foreign to our modern ears, God tells us that celebration is central to pleasing Him; it is central to leading a good life. Modern American life has no time for serious celebrations as did life in centuries past. We've got work to do; projects and deadlines press us. And yet for all our industrial-strength pragmatism, few if any truly important things get accomplished. We have forgotten that celebration isn't just an option; it's a call to full Christian living.

Celebration is worshiping God with our bodies, with the material creation He has set up around us. Celebrating— whether in feasts, ceremonies, holidays, formal worship, or lovemaking—are all part of obeying God's command to "love the Lord thy God with all thine heart, with all thy soul, and with all thy strength" (Deut. 6:5; Mk. 12:30). We are to show our love for God not just with one portion of our being (the spiritual aspect); we are to love God with our whole body, heart and strength and legs and lips.

Complaint is the flag of ingratitude, and it waves above the center of unbelieving hearts—"when they knew God, they glorified him not as God, neither were thankful" (Rom. 1:21). Yet by grace, God's redemption and creation ought to keep us in a perpetual state of thanks which bursts out in celebration at every opportunity.

Throughout Scripture and later history, feasting stands as the central expression of celebration. Through Isaiah, God promised a messianic future in which He would "wipe away tears from off all faces" (Is. 25:8; Rev. 21:4), and He depicts this redemption not in terms of intellectual satisfaction or quiet piety but in terms of an extravagant feast: "And in this mountain shall the LORD of hosts make unto all people a feast of fat things, a feast of wines on the lees, of fat things full of marrow, of wines on the lees well refined" (Is. 25:6)—choice pieces, well-refined wines, and fat things!—all the blessings which anemic moderns say we shouldn't have. Redemption doesn't appear to be a low-cal, cholesterol-free affair.

In addition to redemption, the creation itself calls us to thankfulness. Ancient Greek paganism of the Platonic variety has always despised the created order, seeing matter as a debilitating prison, something to be escaped. But God's creative work has given the material creation a high place—"God saw everything that He had made, and behold it was very good" (Gen 1:31). The apostle Paul tells us "every creature of God is good" (1 Tim. 4:4). Creation is not to be despised. It is a gift of divine art—wheated prairies, royal roses, steep giraffes, cool breezes, etched cliffs, loyal dogs, and tall corn; but also indoor plumbing, plastic toothbrushes, zippers, sourdough bread, Merlot wine, pesto sauces, tri-tip steak, and marinated mushrooms—"nothing is to be refused if it is received with thanksgiving" (1 Tim. 4:4).

To see how far away we are from ancient and medieval notions of celebration, consider what it would take to hold three, week-long celebrations a year as was done in ancient Israel. On top of that, imagine attending several weddings during the year, each of which took a week. Or what would even a three-day feast look like? And it was medieval Christians, long before the Puritans, who understood that the Sabbath was intended to be a feast, not a funeral. That great king, King Alfred (A.D. 849–899), included the following in his Christian law code:

> These days are to be given to all free men: . . . twelve days at Christmas; and the day on which Christ overcame the devil [Feb. 15]; and the anniversary of St. Gregory [Mar. 12]; and the seven days before Easter and the seven after; and one day at the feast of St. Peter and St. Paul [June 29]; and in harvest time the whole week before the feast of St. Mary [Aug. 15]; and one day at the feast of All Saints [Nov. 1]. And the four Wednesdays in the four Ember weeks are to be given to all slaves, to sell to whomsoever they please anything of what anyone has given them in God's name, or of what they can earn in any of their spare time.[1]

Such serious celebrating has molded most eras before our own. We moderns wouldn't know where to start. Yet even if

---

1. Simon Keynes and Michael Lapidge, *Alfred the Great: Asser's Life of King Alfred and Other Contemporary Sources* (New York: Penguin Books, 1983), 170.

we are to try to win back some commitment to celebration, it has to become something we pursue seriously. It won't happen just when we get free time. It has to become a meditation and a discipline, because the crowd is pressing us in the opposite direction.

We can at least start to feast with single meals. But even that will require a concerted pursuit of good cooking and delightful tastes. God has surrounded us with so many amazing tastes, and yet we Americans are barely scratching the surface. The Anglo streak in the American heritage has certainly put a tight squeeze on the breadth of our palates. American food is really so bland and tame we don't even recognize it anymore. And we pass on our picky eating to the next generation. Pure criminality. But even the English know that for good food you have to leave the country. They like France, but the entire world awaits us. We have much to learn from the feastings of Asia and the Latin countries, especially *that land* of feasts—Italy. But feasting is more than celebrating wonderful tastes. Maresca and Darrow note in one of my favorite quotes:

> An Italian meal is not just for allaying hunger. Dining in Italy is an affirmation of the preciousness of simple things—of the worth of bread, of oil, of wine, and of ourselves. It's a rite of renewal, a celebration of human triumph over the daily abrasions that wear us down—the heat of summer, the demands of the job, the indignities of the flu, the indifference of the bureaucracy, the perfidy of inanimate objects. For animals, eating is survival. For humans, eating is a rite of civilization. For Italians, eating is the single great art accessible to us all.[2]

2. Tom Maresca and Diane Darrow, *La Tavola Italiana* (New York: William Morrow and Co., 1988), 17.

Yet it's not just the Italians who understand this truth. The Celtic influence in the Southern United States produces something similar. Andrew Lytle wrote,

> The midday meal, like all meals in the country, has a great deal of form. It is, in the first place, unhurried. Diners accustomed to the mad, bolting pace of cafeterias will grow nervous at the slow performance of a country table. To be late is a very grave matter, since it is not served until everybody is present. . . . Dinner is a social event of the first importance. The family are together with their experiences of the morning to relate; and merriment rises up from the hot, steaming vegetables, all set about the table, small hills around the mountains of meat at the ends, a heaping plate of fried chicken, a turkey, a plate of guineas, or a one-year ham, spiced, and if there is company there, baked in wine; . . . And they eat with eighteenth-century appetites. There is no puny piddling with the victuals, and fancy tin-can salads do not litter the table. . . . His table, if the seasons allow, is always bountiful. The abundance of nature, its heaping dishes, its bulging-breasted fowls, deep-yellow butter and creamy milk, fat beans and juicy corn, and its potatoes flavored like pecans, fill his dining-room with the satisfaction of well-being, because he has not yet come to look upon his produce as so many cents a pound, or his corn at so much a dozen. If nature gives bountifully to his labor, he may enjoy largely.[3]

Good feasting involves drinking too, and central to any biblical feast is wine. Wine itself is quite a miracle. It's something like the birth of a child. A man and woman mix and then create a being wholly distinct from themselves, yet with deep family traits—new and yet the same. A ripe grape

3. Andrew Lytle, "The Hind Tit," in Louis Rubin, *I'll Take My Stand* (Baton Rouge: Louisiana State University Press, 1977), 225–227.

contains two parts, unmarried—an interior sugar juice and an exterior skin full of yeast. But if you marry and mix these parts by crushing a grape, it will start toward creating wine, a third distinct thing, new and yet the same—a "wine that maketh glad the heart of man" (Ps. 104:15). In meditating on Christ's miracle of creating wine, Augustine lamented that we accept the normal creation of wine as any less miraculous, for even as water "turned into wine by the doing of the Lord, so in like manner also is what the clouds pour forth changed into wine by the doing of the same Lord. It has lost its marvellousness by its constant recurrence."[4]

Part of learning to celebrate includes learning how to splurge and not be so tightly utilitarian. Our culture is so wicked in its neglect of savings and its slavery to plastic credit that we, with some right, run the other direction. But if your house is in order, it's time to learn how to splurge at times. Beauty isn't cheap, and neither are artistic meals and good wines. It may not be every week, but we need to learn to splurge with a pure conscience before God. If He has blessed us, then don't we slight Him if we trade that blessing for Top Ramen and boxed wine? There is a time to "bestow that money for whatsoever thy soul lusteth after."

Christ Himself was not one to submit to the false piety behind much tightwad thinking common to evangelicalism. When the woman poured "an alabaster flask of very costly oil" on His head, the immature disciples complained, "'it might have been sold for more than three hundred pence, and have been given to the poor. And they murmured against her.' And Jesus said, 'Let her alone; why trouble ye her? she hath wrought a good work on me. For ye have the poor with you

4. Augustine, "Lectures on the Gospel According to St. John," in *Nicene and Post-Nicene Fathers*, vol. 7, Philip Schaff, ed. (Peabody: Hendrickson Publ., Inc., 1994), 57.

always, and whensoever ye will ye may do them good: but me ye have not always'" (Mk. 14:5–7). *Let her alone.* These are words of liberation.

What more divine gift of celebration do we have than lovemaking? Even those married couples who can't afford to splurge on grand meals and fine wine can feast on each other—"Let him kiss me with the kisses of his mouth: for thy love is better than wine" (Song 1:2). *Holy* Scripture even describes the delight of lovemaking in terms of a feast:

> How fair and how pleasant art thou, O love, for delights! This thy stature is like to a palm tree, and thy breasts to clusters of grapes. I said, I will go up to the palm tree, I will take hold of the boughs thereof: now also thy breasts shall be as clusters of the vine, and the smell of thy nose like apples; And the roof of thy mouth like the best wine for my beloved. (Song 7:6–9)

Yet notice how nonsexual we are in our living. We run from the cold, impersonal sex of our surrounding culture only to act as if lovemaking were some shameful secret. The joy of sexuality doesn't permeate our lives in the way it did in earlier eras. As much as pragmatism characterizes modern life, a living, warm sexuality characterized much medieval living. It was an important category of life, sometimes distorted, but always present. At their best, they knew that God had made them lovemaking creatures, and such passion and natural affection expressed itself in a warm comfortableness with things sexual. That "Puritan" poet Milton described this comfortable sexuality between Adam and Eve.

> [A]nd with eyes
> of conjugal attraction unreprov'd,
> And meek surrender, half-embracing lean'd
> On our first Father, half her swelling Breast
> Naked met his under the flowing Gold

Of her loose tresses hid: he in delight
Both of her Beauty and submissive Charms
Smil'd with superior Love, as Jupiter
On Juno smiles, when he impregns the Clouds
That shed May flowers; and press'd her Matron lip
With kisses pure: aside the Devil turn'd
For envy.[5]

Modernity has not only turned us into shameful animals copulating with strangers, but Christians, who should be the best lovers, the most sexual, are quite stiff and on feverish guard lest anyone actually "commit" a holy kiss. This is a sign of our spiritual immaturity. A more mature Christian culture could honor public etiquette, knowing that lovemaking is a private but not a secret thing, while still leading lives blossoming with celebration of the amazing gifts of sexuality.

But that sort of life has to start with love in the privacy of our marriage beds. We must first pursue celebration there. It ought not merely be a place of satisfying natural urges but a place for delighting in the mysterious beauty of those drives. Why did God delight to entrance us with smooth skin, soft breasts, firm muscles, entangled legs, and slow kisses? There are deep mysteries here, and we love meditating on them in person. Just think, we could be monks of love, devoted to a lifetime of meditation on the realities behind such commands as—"Let thy fountain be blessed: and rejoice with the wife of thy youth. Let her be as the loving hind and pleasant roe; let her breasts satisfy thee at all times; and be thou ravished always with her love" (Prov. 5:18–19).

Like feasts and holidays, celebration in lovemaking is about *remembering*. It is a love of history, a couple's history of good times, of positive personal knowledge shared by no

---

5. John Milton, *Paradise Lost*, Christopher Ricks, ed. (New York: New American Library, 1968), 134, IV.492–503.

others, of refuge from a crazy world. Adulterers despise this sort of history, as do slaves of one-night stands and bitter Christian marriages. Mature Christians love tradition, knowing that their sweet history is the only possible haven for the best lovemaking.

Feasting and lovemaking are only two examples of celebration; others abound, but these two are central. It is our besetting sin to forget God's work for us. How often do we see miserable Christians wasting their half-lives in bitterness, their heads buried firmly in melancholic marriages or soulless busyness, almost enjoying their narrow nitpicking, molding insignificant faults into eternal weapons. "Stand up. Grow up," you want to say. "Life is too short!" and "You have forgotten all the important things in life." Celebration, like good stories, puts things back in perspective. It reminds us of the important things.

So what is it to lead a whole life? How can younger persons live now so that they can look back when they are seventy or eighty and say in all maturity, whether rich or poor, "I have lived well." Most of us, I'm afraid, will look back with decades of regrets, decades of waste, splintered lives. At that age we may finally "have time" to think about the good life, but it will be far too late.

The wisest man in the world taught us that "there is nothing better for a man, than that he should eat and drink, and that he should make his soul enjoy good in his labour. This also I saw, that it was from the hand of God" (Eccl. 2:24). *Nothing better. Nothing* better. Eat, drink, and enjoy the fruit of your labor. "Make your soul enjoy" celebration— feasting on food and love. But doesn't this neglect purist doctrine, social injustice, and more time at the office? Yes, it certainly does.

CHAPTER 8

MOTHER KIRK

Then I wondered what woman this could be to quote such wise words of Holy Scripture; and I implored her, in the name of God, before she left me, to tell me who she was that taught me so kindly.

"I am Holy Church," she replied. "You should recognize me, for I received you when you were a child, and first taught you the Faith. You came to me with godparents, who pledged you to love and obey me all your life."

Then I fell on my knees and besought her mercy, begging her to take pity on me and pray for my sins; and I asked her to teach me plainly how to believe in Christ and the will of Him who created me. "Teach me no more about earthly treasure, O Lady whom men call Holy, but tell me one thing: How may I save my soul?"

—Langland, *Piers Plowman*

Mother fell silent as her sickness took hold of her more strongly. And so on the ninth day of her illness, . . . I closed her eyes; and an immeasurable sorrow flowed into my heart and would have over-flowed in tears. But my eyes under the mind's strong constraint held back their flow, and I stood dry eyed. In that struggle, it went very ill with me.

Modern life has robbed us of so much. Far from much Protestant thinking is the image of the Church as our *mother.*

The ancient prophets often describe the Church in motherly terms (Is. 49; 50; 54; 66:7ff; Jer. 3–4). The book of Revelation depicts the Church as a mother giving birth to the Messiah and then shows her hiding to avoid persecution (Rev. 12). Similarly, the Apostle Paul glories that the "Jerusalem above is free, which is the mother of us all" (Gal. 4:26). The early Protestants were much closer to the ancient and medieval heart on this matter. Calvin encouraged us to

> learn even from the simple title "mother" how useful, indeed how necessary, it is that we should know her. For there is no other way to enter into life unless this mother conceive us in her womb, give us birth, nourish us at her breast, and lastly, unless she keep us under her care and guidance until putting off mortal flesh, we become like angels. Our weakness does not allow us to be dismissed from her school until we have been pupils all our lives. Away from her bosom one cannot hope for any forgiveness of sins or any salvation.[1]

Many modern Christians don't even have a mental drawer in which to file talk about *the Church*, let alone the *Mother* Church. We can speak of churches and the local church and the invisible church, but we don't have a place to speak of the Church. It makes some squeamish. Older Protestants didn't have this problem, but an industrial-strength individualism has beaten our thinking into submission.

As she breathed her last, the child Adeodatus broke out into lamentation, and we all checked him and brought him into silence. But in this very fact, the childish element in me, which was breaking out into tears, was checked and brought into silence by the manlier voice of my mind. For we felt that it was not fitting

---

1. John Calvin, *Institutes of the Christian Religion,* Book IV, John T. McNeill, ed., (Philadelphia: Westminster Press, 1970), 4.

*that her funeral should be solemnized with moaning and weeping
and lamentation. For so it is normal to weep when death is seen
as sheer misery or as complete extinction. But she had not died
miserably, nor did she wholly die.*

Though Scripture pictures the Church in various ways,
the image of a mother is especially helpful for our era. But
what does it mean to speak of the Church as mother? One
way to answer that is to see how Scripture describes moth-
erhood and then look for those traits in the Church. We
regularly turn to Proverbs 31 for a wonderful picture of the
faithful mother. If so, that passage can also fill out the characteristics of the Church.

The Centrality of the Church: In Proverbs 31, mother serves
as the pillar of nourishment and provision—"She brings food
from afar. . . and provides food for her household. . . . She is
not afraid of snow for her household, for all her household
is clothed with scarlet." We get the impression that without
her, the family would collapse. Without her, we would be
hungry and naked and broken. Mother holds life together.

*This great gift also, O my God, my Mercy, You gave Your good
servant, in whose womb You created me, that she showed herself,
wherever possible, a peacemaker between people quarreling and
minds at discord. . . . She was a servant of Your servants. Such of
them as knew her praised, honored, and loved You, O God, in her;
for they felt Your presence in her heart, showing itself in the fruit
of her holy conversation. She had been the wife of one husband,
had requited her parents, had governed her house piously, was
well reported of for her good works.*

The Church should be so central in our thinking that
without her life would collapse. She should play prominently
in our understanding of the past, the present, and the future.
She—not the state or the family or the individual—should
be first on our lips when we discuss evangelism and social

change and the good life. We should turn to the Church first for doctrinal nourishment and practical raiment.

Instead, we ignore mother. We run to the state for social change and licenses. We skip her meals and change her menus. We move our families for "the job" and then only afterward whine that there is no good church around. It's as if mother is just a convenient annex to the household.

What then was it that grieved my heart so deeply? Only the newness of the wound, in finding the custom I had so loved of living with her suddenly snapped short. It was a joy to me to have this one testimony from her: when illness was close to its end, meeting with expressions of endearment such services as I rendered, she called me a dutiful loving son and said in the great affection of her love that she had never heard from my mouth any harsh or reproachful word addressed to herself. But what possible comparison was there, O my God, between the honor I showed her and the service she had rendered me?

Recognizing the centrality of the Church doesn't mean spending more time at the local church (it might mean less). It means that we view the world through medieval eyes— a world where the church spire, not city hall, is the most prominent point on the landscape.

The Authority of the Church: And yet a mother could be central but not authoritative. Children might fawn over mother and say *yes* but then go about their business. Proverbs 31 tells us that mother "opens her mouth with wisdom, and on her tongue is the law of kindness." Proverbs also tells us to "not forsake the law of your mother. Bind them continually upon your heart; tie them around your neck" (6:20–21; cf. 1:8–9).

Like mother, the Church in the Old Covenant had genuine, circumscribed authority (Deut. 17:8–13). This continued in the New, where Christ granted the Church the authority to bind and loose (Mt. 18:18) and teach (Mt. 28:18ff). In Acts, the Church "assembled with one accord" (Acts 15:25) to authoritatively clarify Church teaching, and we have these authoritative teachers "till we all come into the unity of the faith" (Eph. 4:13).

When the day was approaching on which she was to depart this life—a day that You knew though we did not—it came about that she and I stood alone leaning in a window, which looked inwards to the garden. . . . There we talked together, she and I alone, in deep joy; and forgetting the things that were behind and looking forward to those that were before.

We're so American that any talk of genuine Church authority immediately provokes talk of abuses and inquisitions and popes. In an era of thousands of splintered denominations where anyone can hang a church shingle on his own home, worry about Church authority is like lonely orphans stubbornly avoiding Mom. Mom has been thrown out with the bath water; baby sits alone.

We are far more comfortable removing our hat and lowering our eyes for the state than for the Church. Even though the full majesty and fire of the Triune God has determined to bring blessing and cursing through the institution of the Church, we treat the Church with the same deference we give a community bulletin board—a little info, a little humor, a little opportunity.

When the State calls, we scramble to meet its deadlines, write neatly, and say, "Yes, Sir." When the State frowns, we don't just keep driving, thumb our nose at the judge, hop jurisdictions, or make up our own personal constitutions. But when we consider the Church, we think it acceptable to skip around churches as if they were fast food stands. This stand didn't fulfill *my* needs. *We* decide whether they are worthy of *our* money. I decide if the teaching is acceptable.

Because I had now lost the great comfort of her, my soul was wounded and my very life torn asunder, for it had been one life made of hers and mine together. Evodius took up the psalter and began to chant—with the whole house making the response—the psalm Mercy and Judgment I will Sing to Thee, O Lord.

The Church has spoken authoritatively through her creeds. She has passed down centuries of wisdom to us. She has embraced many wise teachers. If she is a mother, then these can't be merely suggestions. They are law until rescinded. Yet a mother's law need not be perfect to be authoritative. And when it needs correcting, individuals have no right to do so as vigilante theologians. How disrespectful. The Church corrects her own creeds. After all, to her alone, not the state, not the family, not Dad, not the parachurch, did Christ give promises of truth and eternal perseverance. And, yes, in those rare, abnormal instances in history where "mother" turns out to be a harlot who murders her children (Lam 1; Hos. 1–4), then God afflicts her for her idolatries (Lam. 1:5) and raises Elijahs and Josiahs for the true mother. But that is not normal Church life.

The Patience of the Church: With wisdom and strength comes patience. Proverbs teaches us that "strength and honor are her clothing; she shall rejoice in the time to come." She may not be able to rejoice at the moment, with all the diapers and infant screams, but she will in the future. She is patient. She knows the frame of her children. Only a tyrannical mother would expect instant maturity and perfection. They have so much to learn, and she is gentle.

I remembered how loving and devout was her conversation with You, how pleasant and considerate her conversation with me, of which I was thus suddenly deprived. And I found solace in weeping in Your sight both about her and for her, about myself and for myself. I no longer checked my tears, but let them flow as they would, making them a pillow for my heart.

Like her husband, Christ, the high priest, the Church should "have compassion on the ignorant, and on them that are out of the way; for that he himself also is compassed with infirmity" (Heb. 5:2). The Church, like a nursery, can be a messy place at times, ripe with the smell of rebellion and ignorance. But we should despise divisions and childish quarrels like warriors despise combat—sometimes battle is necessary, but we should never long for it.

Perfectionism in the Church is very ugly, yet rampant. Calvin complained, "for there have always been those who, imbued with a false conviction of their own perfect sanctity, as if they had already become a sort of airy spirits, spurned association with all men in whom they discern any remnant of human nature." The Lord has called us to be patient with some "doubtful matters" that appear very clear cut, like vegetarianism (Rom. 14:1–3), and He even had patience with Naaman bowing before an idol (2 Kgs. 5:18), and with the heretical disobedience of the Corinthians. Dare we have higher standards than God Himself? Surely we could love truth and draw doctrinal distinctions without having to divide the brethren? "For I desired mercy and not sacrifice" (Hos. 6:6).

Patience should also shape our long-term understanding of Church unity, especially institutional unity. From Abraham's time on, the Church has faced both institutional unity and fragmentation, yet the Church persevered even during apostasy and exile. Roman Catholicism draws many by its evident institutional unity. But that appeal should in no way end the discussion. The Jewish Sanhedrin in the first century had much more institutional unity than the early Christians, but it was apostate. In the Hebraic mindset, institutional unity is no guarantee of covenantal faithfulness. The New Covenant people would face similar troubles as did the Old.

The Apostle Paul raised covenantal threats similar to those of Moses: "if God spared not the natural branches, take heed lest he also spare not thee" (Rom. 11:21).

Many of our early fathers had a far more Hebraic understanding of the Church than does Rome. Jerome tells us that "the church does not consist in walls, but in the truth of her doctrines. The church is there, where true faith is. But fifteen or twenty years ago heretics possessed all walls here, for twenty years ago heretics possessed all the churches here; the church however was where true faith was."[2] Similarly, Hilary teaches us, "I warn you of one thing: beware of Antichrist, for the love of walls has taken you badly; you venerate the church of God badly in houses and buildings. . . . Is it doubtful that Antichrist will have his seat in these?"[3]

Unity is sometimes a veneer for apostasy and fragmentation the scar of faithfulness. Contemporary Protestant fragmentation won't stay with us forever. The Enlightenment joke is growing more stale by the minute. By the Spirit's work in fulfillment of divine promises, the Protestant Church will one day be both faithful and institutionally united. Until then, we have to imitate Elijah's patience.

So let her rest in peace, together with her husband, for she had no other before or after him, but served him, in patience bringing forth fruit for Thee, and winning him likewise for Thee. And inspire, O my Lord my God, inspire Thy servants my brethren, Thy sons my masters, whom I serve with heart and voice and pen,

2. Jerome, *Brevarium in Psalmos* in Jacques Paul Migne, *Patrologiae Latina* (Paris: Garnieri Fratres, 1878); 26.1296 cited in Francis Turretin, *Institutes of Elenctic Theology*, vol. 3 (Phillipsburg: Presbyterian and Reformed Publ., 1997), 54.

3. Hilary, *Contra Arianos, vel Auxentium 12* in Jacques Paul Migne, *Patrologiae Latina* (Paris: Garnieri Fratres, 1878); 10.616 translated in Turretin, *Institutes*, vol. 3, 53.

that as many of them as read this may remember at Thy altar Thy servant Monica.

Monica was the mother of that great Christian—Augustine. She is popularly remembered for her years of prayer for her onetime wayward son, whom God redeemed as one of the greatest gifts to the Christian Church. The above selections are taken from Augustine's memorial to her. Augustine's deep devotion to his mother is a rich image against which we can compare our love for the Mother Church. Do we love the Church? Is she central to our life and community? Do we show respect to her work and heed her pronouncements? Do we hate divisions and long for peace? Do we weep to see her healthy again? Could we really say in her absence, "my soul was wounded and my very life torn asunder"? Surely, Proverbs should haunt us: "a foolish man despises his mother" (Prov. 15:20).

CHAPTER 9

SAYING THE CREEDS

HERITAGE, AUTHORITY, AND THE HIGH PAST

[T]he "pillar and ground" of the Church is the Gospel and the spirit of life; it is fitting that she should have four pillars, breathing out immortality on every side, and vivifying men afresh.

—Irenaeus

The alternative being disaster, the modern evangelical world must soon return to the high past. For some time now we have hyped the importance of having a "contemporary" and "relevant" Christianity, and have done so to the point where we have almost emptied the faith of its historic and orthodox content. To use a phrase from Matthew Arnold, we are "light half-believers in our casual creeds." In a mad pursuit of cisterns that will hold no water, we have come to love the dust on the inside of our empty jars. Our thirst will be a permanent one unless we come back to the creeds of a *historic* Christianity—in particular the Apostles' Creed, the Nicene Creed, and the Definition of Chalcedon.

Once in a conversation with one modern evangelical, I was told that the fathers who handed down these great creeds to us were "just a bunch of guys." This reductionism is typical of modernity and is really the soul and heart of the problem. Of course this modern reductionism has as its evil twin those who profess to love the creeds—do they not mumble them religiously every Sunday?—but in their hearts they are as far away from Christian orthodoxy as the Dalai Lama.

A creedal church is one which thinks, lives, worships, and disciplines in terms of that creed. A creedal church is one in which the words *I believe in God the Father Almighty* provoke tears of gladness in strong men. A creed muttered in nominal unbelief is oxymoronic. The word creed comes from *credo,* "I believe." A creedal church believes certain things to be true, and acts as though truth mattered.

We must remember our heritage. We want to think that forgetting our duties somehow excuses us from our neglect in the performance of them. But in Scripture, forgetting is an additional sin. In our attempt to live creedlessly, we have forgotten the faith of our fathers. We do this because we think our fathers are detached and unconnected from us, and we think this for the trifling reason that these men are all now dead and we never met them.

Our common mentality is that some people came to live around the edges of a pond that we call the "nineties." Others lived around another self-contained pond called the "eighties." That was ten years prior but, as citizens in a mobile society, they have all since moved. In a few years they will all move again, as soon as the trend-spotters down at *Newsweek* tell them to. We call ourselves modern men, but in the memorable words of Andrew Lytle, we are actually *momentary men.*

In the world God created, we actually live on the banks of a great cultural river, and those who live upstream from us affect us in countless ways. For example, even all this foolishness of modernity is still contained by the categories of Chalcedonian orthodoxy, as much as modernist folly rants against it. Consequently, for most modern evangelicals, their sin is not yet really heresy, but rather ingratitude. But the longer we persist in this ingratitude toward our fathers, the closer we drift to actual heresy and apostasy. Significant portions of the evangelical church are already there.

We revolt against historical authority as well. We assume that they had their lives, and we have ours. We are indignant at the thought that our fathers, long since gone from the scene, could possibly have any kind of authority over us. We want to think that the placement of individuals in history is nothing more than a random number sequence, with no authority given to those who came before. But the Lord of all history placed them there, with the command that they leave an inheritance to us. Our duty is to receive that inheritance, build upon it, and become in turn a blessing to our covenantal grandchildren.

Of course objections spring readily to the modern mind. "Does this not set the authority of the Bible aside?" Not at all. The doctrine of *sola Scriptura* insists that the only infallible, ultimate authority is the Bible. Now this short statement which points to the Bible is nowhere found in the Bible, but nonetheless provides us with a fine example of creedal testimony. This short "creed" which tells us to look to the Bible demonstrates how creedal authority should work. A creed should never confess its own authority without simultaneously confessing it as a *lesser* authority.

The Bible tells us that other spiritual authorities exist, but that they are fallible and penultimate. Further, these lesser spiritual authorities are not just "allowed," they are inescapable. The question is not *whether* we will have them, but *which* of them we will have. We do not understand that when we have removed all traces of Nicean orthodoxy, this does not leave us standing in a fresh meadow with a newly-discovered Bible, but rather with the ethereal magisterium of the latest heretical balloon juice cooked up at the Christian

Booksellers Association, which never met a wind of doctrine it didn't like.

Repentance will bring with it a love for the high past. That love will lead to a more thorough acquaintance with the men there—from Polycarp to Athanasius, from Irenaeus to Augustine, we will come to respect and honor those men who taught our brothers and sisters, and in so doing left a testimony that teaches to this day. Part of this testimony is their crucial contribution to the formation of the glorious creeds.

So, had enough of theological fads and fashions? Are you sick of that Aerobics with the Angels class on Wednesday nights? Are you tired of sermons that trifle with the truth? Does your skin crawl when you walk through an evangelical bookstore? Are you weary of the constant irrelevance of contemporary relevance? Then welcome to evangelical orthodoxy.

I believe in God the Father Almighty; Maker of heaven and earth. In giving this particular creedal testimony, in this particular way, we take a stand as historic Christians. We are not to confess our faith in isolation, but rather in concert with other saints throughout the world, and down through the history of the Church.

Together with them, we believe in God the Father Almighty. The God of the Bible is not some limp-wrist divinity. He is Almighty, and it comforts us to know that this omnipotent One is our Father. He is not a vague Benevolence; He is the king of all glory and nothing is too difficult for Him. At the same time, we confess He is our Father. As the Almighty One, the distance between us and Him is infinite.

Because He is the Maker of heaven and earth, we did not come about as the result of primordial forces working manfully away on a pile of primordial goo. We were created, *imago Dei,* by the same One who made everything in heaven and on earth, by the simple word of His power. As John the apostle stated, nothing that was made was made apart from Him.

We are Christians; we know that Jesus Christ our Lord is the *only-begotten* Son of the Father. This refers to His unique status as one who never began to be the Son of God. The relationship between Father and Son is an eternal one, just as the author of Hebrews teaches us. There was never a time when He was not. Jesus Christ is eternally-begotten of the Father. This is the One whom we confess as our Lord. To confess another lord is to fall short of salvation.

Everything about the beginning of His incarnation was miraculous, from His conception to his birth of a virgin. At the end of His life, Jesus died and was buried during the rule of a particular governor of Judea. These things are no myth; they were not done in a corner. The manner of His death and burial was in full accordance with the Scriptures. The cross, burial and resurrection are the heart of the gospel. He rose from the dead *physically*. A spirit does not have flesh and bone as Jesus did, and still does. Christ the Lord is enthroned today at God's right hand. As the psalmist says, He will remain there until all His enemies are subdued and placed beneath His feet. At the end of history, Christ will judge all men. God has declared that Christ is the Judge of all by bringing Him back from the dead.

The Holy Spirit is the third person of the Trinity and has all the divine attributes held by both the Father and the Son, and in His power He binds together the holy catholic Church. In part, we make this confession because we share the communion of this Church with every true saint throughout all history. In the heart of the new covenant, at the center of this communion, we find forgiveness of sins. If there is no forgiveness, we all need to give up, because we are all lost.

As Christians, we do not hold to the immortality of the soul, but rather to the resurrection of the dead. We will live forever as sons and daughters of God—in the *body*. This life forever is the grace of God, a grace which will never cease.

As this summary of the Apostles' Creed makes clear, the ancient creeds have done much to shape the expression of our common faith. In a similar way, Nicea and Chalcedon give us a time-tested way to confess the truth of God as it is found in Christ. The language of these creeds is formal, lofty, scriptural, and Christ honoring. In these creeds, we find clear testimony to the heart of the gospel—the cross and burial, the resurrection and ascension, the enthronement of Christ, and His Second Coming in power and glory. This gospel is always to be understood as what God did for us in Christ, and not what we do by some act of our own will.

These creeds were born in controversy, and we take the answers for granted now, but when they were under dispute, the future of all Christendom was in the balance. Further, the history of the creeds shows us the idea of creedal advance. The Church grows and matures doctrinally over time. Some wonderful creedal and confessional statements have been made since the time of these early confessions, but only by portions of the Church. The Canons of Dort and the Westminster Confession are wonderful examples of the kind of doctrinal maturity which is possible—but creeds of this caliber have not yet been confessed by the Church universally. A central part of our duty is to labor and pray for the time when the entire Church is mature enough to confess a truly Reformed faith, reformed according to Scripture.

But we are not yet in a position to press on. Part of the reason why creedal advance has stalled in our generation is that we have seriously neglected those truths which the Church *has* confessed universally. Such agreement provides the only possible foundation for building further. The Church, no less than individuals, needs to live up to what it has already attained.

But for the modern evangelical, who does not believe in creeds, this is all too much. He has no respect for ecclesiastical history, or for the sovereign providence of God over all history. And so he wants none of it—he does not believe it. And if he knew a little Latin, he could begin his denial with *non credo,* which in its short, succinct way, is a nice little creed. In the world God made, we must either affirm or deny.

But he may continue to protest. He does not believe in creeds because he does believe in the Bible—the Bible only. Isn't this the classical Protestant doctrine of *sola Scriptura?* Not exactly. There is no refuge from the necessity of creeds. When a man opens his Bible, the first thing he encounters— the table of contents—is a creed. When a man looks at the spine and sees the letters NIV, NASB, KJV, he is gazing upon a very small creed. Because the Church is the pillar and ground of the truth, the Church must testify concerning the truth. Even the man who says he has no truck with creeds and wants to stick with the Bible alone, must say that this book and not that one is "the Bible alone."

The same principle even extends to the matter of Bible translations. The Church is the guardian of the truth. The Church must say this translation is correct, not that one, or the Church must say (as it is doing today) that it doesn't really matter. The wielding of ecclesiastical authority in these matters is inescapable; the only question is whether the authority will be used in a way to build the saints up, or tear them down.

As we return to the medieval mindset, this means it is necessary to return to a translation of the Bible which, to use an older phrase, is "approved to be read in the churches." We must return to a translation which is, in some recognizable sense, *creedal.* The selection of a Bible translation should not be considered a matter of individual choice. In the English-speaking world, this has to mean the King James Version of the Bible. Remember, the creeds are to be understood as the common confession of the *Church,* and not determined by the individual purchases of Bible buyers.

Of course we first need to resolve the issue of names—the most common name for the translation defended here is the one already used—the King James Version, or KJV. Another name for it, and a far better one, is the Authorized Version, or AV. One of the great ironies of history is how King James I, a blasphemous sodomite, managed to get his name attached to the most widely-used English version of the Bible, and the sooner we get his name off of there the better we should like it.

But the names are the easy part. Substantively, three central issues are involved. The first has to do with manuscript tradition, the second with translation philosophy, and the third with ecclesiology. Before any translation is acclaimed as "just what we need," we should want it to be translated from the right manuscript tradition, which most modern versions are not. It should be translated well, which most modern versions are not. But most importantly, the whole endeavor should be conducted under the auspices of the Church. The first two issues are of course very important, but are outside the scope of this book. The third issue—that of Church authority—must be settled before we have any reasonable chance of getting the first two right.

Martyn Lloyd-Jones once said, "Any study of church history, and particularly any study of the great periods of revival or reawakening, demonstrates above everything else just this one fact: that the Christian Church during all such periods has spoken with authority." The Word of God speaks with authority. Whenever men abandon that Word, they frequently want the Church to speak authoritatively in her *own* voice, supplanting the Word with the traditions of men. But this does not make Church authority suspect, for when the Church is governed by the authority of the Word, the Church speaks authoritatively as well . . . but not like the scribes. God in His Word always speaks a sure word in a slippery place. When we are mastered by that Word, we will learn to speak the same way as well. "The disciple is not above his master: but every one that is perfect shall be as his master" (Lk. 6:40).

But in the modern world, authority of any kind is a dirty word. True authority is written off as arrogance, but this simply shows how the arrogance of individualism dislikes any organized competition. Authority is built into the world. In any given situation, someone is going to wield authority; someone is going to make the call. Our concern should be to place that authority in the place where Scripture places it. When it comes to the oracles of God, that authority has been given to a faithful Church.

But this authority must be explained. The position of historic Protestants is that the Word of God is self-authenticating. This means that it does not need the Church to authenticate it. As the Westminster Confession says, "The authority of the Holy Scripture, for which it ought to be believed, and obeyed, dependeth not upon the testimony of any man, or Church; but wholly upon God (who is truth itself), the author thereof: and therefore it is to be received, because it is the Word of God."[1] But if this is the case, then what does

1. *Westminster Confession of Faith*, I.4.

it mean to say that the Church has declared certain books canonical, or that the Church has declared a certain textual family to be the one which God preserved throughout history? To many it appears that such confessional Protestants are trying to suck and blow at the same time. They want the Bible to be self-authenticating, and yet they want to be able to tell people authoritatively what books are in the Bible. So which will it be?

The question springs from a misunderstanding of the nature of Church authority. The Church must claim no authority of any kind over the text of Scripture itself, and yet the Church must *creedally* acknowledge the canon of Scripture and the text of Scripture—which, incidentally, should be the *textus receptus,* the text underlying the Authorized Version. But how is this possible?

Authority is being exercised, but it is not authority over the self-authenticating text of Scripture. The authority is being exercised in the household of God and over spurious writings. Consider the latter case of spurious writings first. If someone were to claim that the Book of Mormon, for example, is the Word of God, the true Church of Christ has the full authority to reject it as a merely human composition. To authoritatively reject that which is *not* Scripture is the necessary counterpart of submissively accepting that which is Scripture. If something is *not* the Word of God, the Church has the authority to say so.

The Church also has authority in the teaching of her ministers, and in the lives of the people. The Bible grants authority to the Church, an authority which must maintain godly discipline within the ranks of the ministry and eldership. If a pastor begins to claim that 2 Peter was written by a pious fraud in the second century, when the Church removes him from his position, the Church is not exercising authority over 2 Peter. The authority is being exercised over a man, and the standard being used is a recognized canon which provides the standard (or *kanon*) for discipline.

But when it comes to church authority, moderns are trained to be immediately suspicious—any exercise of authority must be a creeping tyranny. In many churches, this distrust of authority is so far advanced that effective church discipline has become impossible. The medieval mind knows better. While true authority refuses to "lord it" over God's people, true authority will nevertheless speak without stuttering. "This is the Word of God, and that is not." Does this pronouncement *make* something into the Word of God? Certainly not—to use Luther's example, when John the Baptist pointed to the Lamb of God, and testified, he was not making Jesus the Lamb of God. He was simply recognizing the truth.

A return to medieval thinking is a return to creedal thinking—and not just limited to those symbols recognized as formal creeds. A return to a creedal mind will come to see, gladly, the implicit creeds which shape our expressions of faith. But the modern evangelical church does not want this voice of authority. The modern evangelical church wants the doctrinal structure of an inner tube and the stability of a bowl of pudding.

CHAPTER 10

A GOOD WIFE AND WELCOMING HEARTH

RECOVERING THE FAMILY . . . AGAIN

> A genial hearth; a hospitable board,
> And a refined rusticity.
>
> —Wordsworth

Many have taken up the lament over the disintegration of the modern family. Those concerned with traditional values point to the signs of the familial times, whether great or small. We see burgeoning divorce rates, no common meals, children without fathers, hours facing the tube instead of one another, marriages with double incomes and no kids, the widespread practice of abortion, sodomite marriages, and so forth. When such things are considered, the lament is not at all surprising. As with many other aspects of our modern lives, we are used to the lamentations as a well-rehearsed accompaniment to the decay. But perhaps the problem is not the disintegration of the modern family. Perhaps the problem is the modern family.

We too often forget that in a world in which both good and evil exist, virtue cannot be found in a transitive verb. It is not enough to be told that a man loves, we want to know what he loves. If another man is tolerant, we do not know if this is virtuous or not. What does he tolerate? The same

problem exists with the verb *"conserve."* To say that someone is a conservative does not tell us what he is interested
in conserving. Within our lifetimes, we have seen hard line
communists trying to conserve the Soviet Union, fanatical
Muslims trying to conserve ancient Islamic traditions, and
American right-wingers trying to conserve the rich heritage
of "Ozzie and Harriet." The word in itself does not communicate very much.

Now many of our contemporaries who are concerned
about the future of the modern family are really interested
in conserving that family the way it was before the impossi-
bility of modernism's social experiment became evident. Put
another way, we are not really interested in reaping what we
have sown, which makes our current situation unpleasant.

Families are not voluntary arrangements under our authority, to be altered at our evanescent whims and pleasures.
The various ways in which the modern family has been dis-
integrating tell us a great deal about what it was like before
it began to fall apart. Once a problem has become glaring,
modern conservatives all too often simply want to call us
back to the *status quo ante*—i.e., the way it was right before
our problems became obvious. They want to return to that
pleasant and tranquil time when the hurricane was still over
the horizon, invisible and gathering force. We did not understand our danger, we were not preparing for anything, but it
was nice and the sun was shining.

In the mindset concerning marriage proposed here, the
point is not to analyze *our* practices in marriage, or even what
our grandparents did. We will not get back to our point of
departure if we are only willing to retrace just a few steps.
Our desire should be to consider what marriage in its essence
is. How were we created to function in the beginning? What
did God require of us when He made us male and female?

And further, was this pattern ever seen and practiced in the history of the Church?

Our modern fascination with marriage is not an indication of health, but rather quite the reverse. We are interested in the subject the way a four-hundred pound man is interested in dieting. The volume of material we publish on the subject of marriage and family is simply phenomenal. We have seminars, books, study guides, weekends, romantic cruises, and all the rest of it. And although much of it is trite, misplaced, or compromised, a good deal of the advice that is given is consistent with Scripture, and it is not our purpose to quarrel with the good advice which may be contained there. But however much we bustle around the edges of this subject, we will not recover our marital senses until we return to certain foundational issues and address them clearly and without apology.

To come to the point, marriage is not an egalitarian institution. The Lord has determined, and has told us plainly, that the husband is the head of his wife. Through His apostle, He compared the marriage relation to that of Christ serving as the head of the Church. We, in the grip of modernity's individualism, think that means that the husband is supposed to be in charge. We believe that Paul was telling us that the man is "the boss." As a result, we have on the one hand a feminist reaction against this "truth" and on the other a fundamentalist macho-man embracing of it. But what this biblical teaching really means is that marriage is *federal.* Communicating this is difficult because our most common use of the word is limited to references to our federal government which is (in its essence) as anti-federal as can be imagined. We have not only lost the concept, we have destroyed the words which could enable us to recover it.

The word *federal* comes from the Latin word *foedus*, which means *covenant*. A federal government should therefore be, on the face of it, a government by covenant. The recovery of federal marriage is therefore obviously related to a right understanding of what has come to be called *covenant theology*, which emphasizes in its doctrinal standards something called *federal headship*. The more systematic formulations of this theology grew out of the Reformation, but the central features of it were deeply embedded in medieval and feudal life. It is important to note, however, that the discussion is not about this particular doctrine or that one, or whether a certain teaching is affirmed, but rather whether or not certain covenantal assumptions govern. When they do, it results in a certain way of *thinking*. That way of thinking provides the only real alternative to the modern family and all its troubles.

The doctrine of federal headship teaches that Jesus Christ is a federal head of all His people, in the same way that Adam was the federal head of the entire human race. In the fifth chapter of Romans, the apostle devotes a great deal of time to a comparison of these two Adams—these two covenant heads. When Adam was making his choice in the garden, he was not just another individual. He did not approach the tree of the knowledge of good and evil as one of the guys. If that is all he were, then of course to condemn the entire race for his behavior would have been a gross injustice. The fact that this charge is commonly made illustrates how our individualist age thinks of Adam as someone who could be looked up in a phone book. But as a federal head, *he was the entire human race.* Put another way, we were all there, in him.

Our salvation came to us in the same way. Christ is the head of His people, and His obedience to God is reckoned as ours. Of course, as the Lord, He is "in charge" of the

Christian church. But the point is much richer than this. Covenantally speaking, He *is* the Christian church. We are Christians because we are in Christ.

Now, Christian husbands are commanded to love their wives in this way, with this understanding. The command clearly goes far beyond, "Be nice to your wife. Take her on dates." The husband is to represent her, and all the children she gives him as a covenant head. Each home is to be a small republic, with a representative head who represents that family, and who in a covenantal sense is that family. But the modern family, even when it has not disintegrated, insists upon functional parity between husband and wife. But despite what we think, a husband is a head and a lord—his fiefdom may be tiny, and he is frequently not worthy of it. In the modern world he is almost certainly confused about it. Be that as it may, the facts of the case are unaltered. He is the covenant head of the household, and his refusal to acknowledge it will only make him a poor head, not a non-head.

Our mother Sarah served her husband with this understanding, calling him her lord. As moderns, we have many reasons for rejecting this teaching, but all of them share in common a mischaracterization of those who do not reject it—however few of them there may be. For example, the doctrine of headship and submission is easily characterized as dogma fitted only for megalomaniacal men and women of very little brain. This modernist caricature is thought to be biblical—both by those who reject it and by those who in the name of some kind of traditionalism accept it. But counter examples come easily to mind. Abigail was a woman of great ability, intelligence, and beauty. She also was a woman of gracious and humble submission. As she spoke to the servants of David when he summoned her to be his wife, "Behold, let thine handmaid be a servant to wash the feet of the servants of my lord." We can only write Abigail off as an uneducated scullery maid if we ignore everything else the scriptural account tells us of her greatness.

C. S. Lewis commented on this pattern as he explained humility and hierarchy to modernists who are trying, although perhaps not very hard, to make out a language they do not know.

> Portia wished that for Bassanio's sake, she might be trebled "twenty times herself." "A thousand times more fair, ten thousand times more rich," and protests that, as things are, "the full sum of her is sum of nothing," "an unlesson'd girl." It is prettily said and sincerely said. But I should feel sorry for the common man, such as myself, who was led by this speech into the egregious mistake of walking into Belmont and behaving as though Portia really *were* an unlessoned girl. A man's forehead reddens to think of it. She may speak thus to Bassanio: but *we* had better remember that we are dealing with a great lady.[1]

Egalitarianism may be seen and understood as the very skeletal structure of modernity. It can be found everywhere, even in those who profess to stand against it. One of the reasons it has this ubiquitous presence is because it is one of the most striking features of the modern home—and the home is the molecule which builds every larger culture. In that home, we have lost the idea of office. We see every relationship as a competition or struggle for power between individuals. The man has his perspective and the woman hers. With this assumption we then see the scriptural requirement of submission as though God weighs in on the side of the males. We believe it is saying that whenever there is a disagreement, the man as *an individual* gets his way.

1. C. S. Lewis, *A Preface to Paradise Lost* (London: Oxford University Press, 1942), 120.

But this is not the sense at all. The man is an individual, a private person, but *as husband* he also holds a public office. He is invested with this office; he is called to wear a metaphorical robe. He and his wife are both individual citizens of this small republic, and they each have their individual perspectives. But he is also a public person, and is called to function in that role as the representative head of his household. In a very important sense, he *is* that household. It is this sense of familial identification which modern men have lost.

In Shakespeare's *Henry V*, we see a mode of expression which reveals this understanding in a medieval form—an understanding which, frankly, is entirely alien to modern modes of thinking. Although this example is taken from the civil realm, the illustration of applied federal thinking is a good one. After the great victory of Henry over the French forces at Agincourt, the king of France greets him in this fashion. "Right joyous are we to behold your face, most worthy brother England; fairly met: so are you, princes English, every one."[2] Henry was far more than just one man in England. And even as a king, he was considered more than simply the most important man in England. Mark Twain's *Connecticut Yankee* notwithstanding, the simple idea of being the "boss" was not the medieval idea of lordship. In a fundamental, representative sense, Henry *was* brother England.

Now this idea of federal headship is foundational to marriage. Modern marriage seeks to build on another foundation altogether. Because this is a revolt against reality, against the way the world is, the real foundation cannot be torn up. But in our misconception, our belief that another foundation is an option, we can fail to build on it properly. When we revolt against God's world, we must not be surprised when His

2. *Complete Works of Shakespeare* (Roslyn: Walter Black, Inc., 1937), 562.

world wins. Our efforts are futile and will not change the way things are. We may hurt ourselves in the attempt, but the attempt will not achieve its end. We may tire ourselves out throwing snowballs at the sun. As we lie there exhausted, perhaps we will reflect, and learn wisdom.

When understood in a household, the applications of this foundational truth, not surprisingly, can be found everywhere. And at every point, they will reveal how much this knowledge of headship and submission is completely out of step with the spirit of the age. The points of contrast and collision will occur as frequently inside the Church as outside it—for tragically, most of the Church has struck a truce with modernity.

One example should suffice. We have accepted, as a self-evident truth in both church and state, that women should have the right to vote. We believe *this* because we think it was unfair that only men used to be able to vote. We believe this because we think that, back in our dark ages, men used to vote as individuals, and that women as individuals were considered too silly to be able to vote. They were not to trouble their little heads about it, and this condescension was of course reckoned to be inflammatory. So we all took to the barricades; women were granted the right to vote, and the sound of triumph was great in the land.

Put in plain terms, suppose that William Thompson is married to Susan Thompson. Suppose further that a decision is to be made within a local church and the thing is to be brought to a vote. Our assumption is that under the *ancien regime* the patriarchs wouldn't care what Susan thought but did want to discover what William thought for some reason. So they asked him. We are more enlightened, and so we ask them both.

But the medieval assumption is that we should find out what the *Thompsons as a household* think. We should discover this by asking the spokesman, the federal head. He would answer for his family, and in speaking, represent them. In other words, the issue is not whether men vote as opposed to women. The issue is whether families can vote. In our modernist blindness and folly, we did not enfranchise women; we disenfranchised the household. And consider where it has gotten us. When husbands and wives agree, voting the same way, all we have done is multiply the entire vote tally by two. And when they disagree, all that has happened is that their votes cancel out the voice of their household.

Of course this teaching, like all doctrine in a fallen world, is susceptible to abuse. A man who walks on the earth God gave him may stumble and fall. But a man who seeks to prevent this temptation by walking on water will meet with little improvement. We are to prevent the abuse by doing what we are told. Our Lord taught us that the first will be last, and the last first. He said that the greatest would be the servant of all. He said, in so many words, that the way up is down. Many men and women are grasping after some sort of fulfillment in their relationships, and it is not surprising they do not find it. They fail because they want to build their marriages on their own terms, on the basis of what *they* want. But the center of the family is the marriage union between the husband and wife. As a union which pictures Christ and His bride, the Church, marriage is designed to glorify God. The chief end of marriage, like the chief end of man, is to enjoy God and glorify Him forever. Marriage is what He made of it. It will never be whatever we might wish it to be.

Modernity has abandoned the household gods, not because we have rejected the idolatry as all Christians must, but because we have rejected the very idea of the household.

We no longer worship Vesta, but have only turned away from her because our homes no longer have any hearths. Now we worship Motor Oil. If our rejection of the old idols were Christian repentance, God would bless it, but what is actually happening is that we are sinking below the level of the ancient pagans. But when we turn to Christ in truth, we find that He has ordained every day of marriage as a proclamation of His covenant with the Church. A man who embraces what is expected of him will find a good wife and a welcoming hearth. He who loves his wife loves himself.

So suppose a woman were to tell her husband that he was like a medieval king to her. Such things are awkward for urbane moderns to say and hear—we believe people who think this way are trying to live in some fantasy world—sort of a marital *Dungeons and Dragons.* We believe that to take pleasure in such comments is simply a cheesy attempt to put a little fire in the romantic relationship by playing at knights and castles, damsels and unicorns. But there are realities here which cannot be so easily dismissed. She should know the importance of what she does, and he should reckon it to be among the permanent things.

CHAPTER 11

NURTURING FAT SOULS

LOVING CHILDREN THROUGH STORIES

The most important parts of faithful child rearing are invisible and intangible. We can never figure them out by calculations or churn them out in neat, mechanical, step-by-step processes. They are wisdom, not knowledge. And God doesn't just expect us to grasp the ungraspable for our own peace and fun, but for the working out of all of His purposes throughout history. That's quite a task before us as we stare at our troops—troops wild with jam-smeared faces and milk moustaches.

The Old Testament closes by promising that in the New, "He shall turn the heart of the fathers to the children, and the heart of the children to their fathers, lest I come and smite the earth with a curse" (Mal. 4:6). This reference to "turning the heart" suggests much more than just raising good, obedient children who don't talk back or do drugs. That's relatively easy. Good Christian communities (a minority) are full of decent kids, and those millions of evangelicals who haven't arrived at that level yet need to stop there first. Spanking mechanics and parental authority are "first principles" that we should have learned long ago (Heb. 5:12).

But we should want much more than just decent children. Rather than failing at basic discipline, I'm much more worried about raising decent but soulless children, children with that blank, unconscious stare who run in tight grooves, completely lacking in any passion for anything grand and beautiful. It seems that decent but soulless children and their parents would be those to whom much was given and much was buried.

"Soul" is one of those real but intangible characteristics that we can easily point to, though it won't squeeze through a scientific screen. The more biblical synonym for this sense of soul is "wisdom," and we can say that a soulful person is one who is *consciously* aiming to absorb the truths of the books of Proverbs, Psalms, Ecclesiastes, and Song of Solomon. None of us is there yet, since it's a lifetime pursuit. But some ignore the path entirely, and others look at it disdainfully. And those are the people who will have to give an account for their soulless kids.

But here again, we are too comfortable with the biblical word "wisdom." We hear it, think we grasp it, and run down the line. We think the message of wisdom in Proverbs is just "no debt, no gossip, no proud looks." But Pharisees can do those things. Wisdom or having soul involves so much more. It is an active, conscious pursuit (Prov. 2:2) that creates a "fountain of life" (Prov. 13:14) and a "tree of life" (Prov. 3:18) and "life unto thy soul" (Prov. 3:22). It creates a life that aims to gush with joy and blossom with creativity. It eats its bread with joy and drinks its wine with a merry heart; for God has accepted its works (Eccl. 9:7).

But it is even more than that. Wisdom involves wonder, a mysterious, humble wonder—a taste for beauty: "There be three things which are too wonderful for me, yea, four which I know not: the way of an eagle in the air; the way of a serpent upon a rock; the way of a ship in the midst of the sea; and the way of a man with a maid" (Prov. 30:18–19). This sort of soul doesn't get stuck in the modern, efficient, pragmatic game that blinds us to the wonder around us; it can stop and be amazed at flying, slithering, sailing, and sexuality.

Such is a hint of a "fountain of life," a soulful living. But how can we nurture it in our children? How can we encourage this exuberant wisdom?

The story of childrearing is almost wholly about imitation. We do good or ill, and the young ones follow in lock step, no matter how much we talk and point elsewhere. They are designed that way. We laugh sometimes at the strong physical resemblance between parents and children, but, even without that, children carry over their parents' exact facial expressions, voice cadences, and personality quirks. How many adults swore to themselves as teenagers they would never do certain things their parents did, only to find themselves reincarnating the very same behavior. Even the myths of rebellion confirm this. Moderns tend to believe that "teenage" rebellion is something created *ex nihilo,* completely at odds with parental values. But watch closely. Such rebellion is just more imitation of the parents' own more subtle rebellion. Hot-tempered parents nurture hot-tempered teenagers. Pessimistic, negative parents mold pessimistic, negative children. Apathetic parents give us . . . and so on. As painful as it may be to hear, rebellion is almost always the parents' own personalities reflecting themselves.

This inescapable imitation should be listed as a means of growing in grace. Parents often jest about their children being "means of sanctification," suggesting that child rearing is often a trial. But the situation is much more serious than a passing trial. Given the way children have to imitate parents (or whoever fills that role), one cannot just coast passively, selfishly, like we often do through tough times. Our tiniest daily responses in front of the kids constantly mold and chip away at their persons. Children are a means of sanctification because they are *daily* adopting their parents' characters, virtues and vices and all. This is a blessing when we are faithful, but it's a frightening mirror when we see our own sins growing in them. With kids around, we can't just move slowly on our own growth. We have to grow in grace *for the sake of the kids.* If we don't, then we can become a curse to them and their children.

If we want our children to be soulful fountains of life, then we must live it first ourselves. We have to be absorbing the life of wisdom too. And we can't fake it, just talking about full lives. Children have scopes that can detect hypocrisy instantly.

Developing a soulful life requires great diligence. The key requirement in nurturing our children so that they *want* to pursue it themselves is that they trust us. If they don't trust us, we can't lead them. This is easy with very little ones, but it requires greater work as they grow older. If they trust, they won't rebel in difficult times, and they will want to follow our positive model.

How do we develop trust? The best way is for parents to seek to imitate the Lord's own example. He gives us a perfect model for nurturing loyalty. In part, He draws our loyalty by His sacrifice, His intimate knowledge of us, and His love of beauty.

Sacrifice: We know that "the goodness of God" leads us to repentant trust (Rom. 2:4). And God's goodness is centered most clearly in His sacrifice: "Greater love hath no man than this, that a man lay down his life for his friends" (Jn. 15:13). How much more does this apply to our children? If we aren't willing to sacrifice our lives for the nurture of our children, then we shouldn't even proceed. We don't love them with the greatest love possible. But again, contemporary Christian talk cheapens this. Every minimal parent would agree to martyring their physical life for their kids. But Christ didn't just die a physical death. He surrendered His personal glory for our good, making "himself of no reputation" and taking "upon him the form of a servant" (Phil. 2:7). We talk of our willingness to die for the children, but are we willing to sincerely sacrifice careers and vacations and personal talents for their sakes *without bitterness?* The whole orientation of our household must be focused on sacrificing for our children. This is a sign of deep love.

Intimacy: The Lord not only draws our trust by sacrifice, He also does it by intimacy, by personal knowledge. He knows the number of the hairs on our heads, but also "the desires of thine heart" (Ps. 37:4), our passions and hopes and how they can all blend together for good. No child will be inspired to trust a parent who has only a "too busy," superficial concern for him. They flourish with our intimacy, especially with times all alone with one parent. When they are all grown, if they love our Lord, they do so because they love the love they saw in us. Arguments, proofs, and apologetics may have their place, but not in nurturing deep trust. They will imitate what they find lovely. If our lives are not lovely, then our children will pursue someone or something else's loveliness.

Pursuing Beauty: It is this attraction to loveliness that lies at the heart of nurturing soul. God has made us to be drawn to the beautiful. So often the divide between children who have full souls and those who don't lies here with the pursuit of beauty. The serious pursuit of beauty, for both children and adults, has a delightfully amplifying effect on all other areas of life. It makes us better at everything else, whether that be theology, engineering, homemaking, or plumbing. The connection here is quite mysterious, but it's often quite radical. Poetry, music, and fiction can utterly transform the coldest logician, computer programmer, or colonel into someone with soul.

Imagine how powerfully we can nurture soul in our children by leading them in beauty from infancy. And we can't just force them ahead of us, such as piano lessons just for the sake of discipline. We need to lead them in love for the goal. We need to lead them in a passion for beautiful music in a way that they want to delight in it themselves.

Children should be almost criminal in their love of stories. If they aren't regularly begging you for stories, even after you seem to have been reading all day, then something may be wrong with them. They live and grow by means of narrative, especially fiction. Families and schedules differ, but our family, like a growing number of Christian families, reads passages from one to three books (fiction, history, theology, or Scripture) at every meal, making sure that we begin the day with plenty of poetry. Meals are especially important for families, since they naturally display sacrifice, intimacy, and beauty.

Stories frame a child's interior life for living in this world. Fiction is far more realistic than we realize. Fiction and poetry mysteriously transfer truth in a far more powerful way than anything else. God Himself chose to write in passionate poetry and narrative and parables rather than in the bureaucratic style of a systematic theology. But again, parents have to lead the way. Many parents, however, have little taste for fiction, though they allow it for the "little kids." Some parents disdain fiction because they are bony pragmatists, not having the time, but others even claim that it is unspiritual ("I just want Scripture"). Though I couldn't prove it in an ecclesiastical court, I'm beginning to suspect that parents who don't enjoy fiction must have some serious spiritual problem lurking about, either in a very distorted view of spirituality or in a rejection of beauty. They are like the person who ungratefully refuses to delight in God's handiwork in nature. Time will tell in the lives of their children.

Though our modern heads may cringe at the wording, Proverbs tells us that "the liberal soul shall be made fat" (Prov. 11:25). That is a good way to summarize everything above. We want fat-souled children. We want them to have full, faithful lives—joyful, balanced, and lovely. But wisdom doesn't happen passively. It takes a diligent household and constant prayer, but with that He promises that "the soul of the diligent shall be made fat" (Prov. 13:4). That should be our prayer: Lord enable us to raise children with fat souls. "He that putteth his trust in the Lord shall be made fat" (Prov. 28:25).

CHAPTER 12

SWORDS INTO PLOWSHARES

AGRARIAN CALM AND CLOSE TO THE SOIL

> My wife and I have what I've earned by honest toil alone; and she shall share it among my daughters and my dear children. For though I should die this very day, my debts are all paid, and I've always returned what I've borrowed, before going to bed. . . . It is common sense that every man must work, either by ditching or by digging, or by travailing in prayer—the active or the contemplative life—for such is God's will. And according to Psalm 128, a man who lives by his own honest labor is blessed in body and soul—"for thou shalt eat the labors of thine hands: O well is thee, and happy shalt thou be."
>
> —Langland, *Piers Plowman*

"Evil company corrupts good habits," and so can the city. We understand how the people surrounding us can mold us for good or ill, but we often fail to see how radically our local world—roads, homes, and codes—can influence our growth in holiness. Those of us who have abandoned the city for the country, or vice versa, know quite poignantly these opposed worlds. The differences often go quite deep, quite beyond the stereotypical dramas which capture the honest country simpleton stumbling through Manhattan. These deeper but subtler differences involve rhythms and bonds and silence.

And it is here where Christianity speaks vividly to questions of culture and community.

A long tradition, firmly rooted in Vergil's delightfully agrarian poems, the *Georgics*, argues for the superiority of country over city life, of farm over skyscraper, of agrarianism over industrialism. This tradition includes not only Vergil's ancient Roman love of the virtues of country life, but also Langland's medieval allegory, *Piers Plowman*, through to the influential Southern agrarians of the twentieth century— Lytle, Penn Warren, Tate, Davidson, and Weaver.

One of the common themes in this literature is an antipathy to that prime product of industrialism—the city. It is the city, we hear, that gathers all the worst features of modern life—alienation, irresponsibility, violence, consumerism, pseudo progress, and social coddling. In this vein, the Southern agrarian, John Crowe Ransom wrote,

> Industrialism is an insidious spirit, full of false promises and generally fatal to establishments since, when it once gets into them for a little renovation, it proposes never again to leave them in peace. Industrialism is rightfully menial, of almost miraculous cunning but no intelligence; it needs to be strongly governed or it will destroy the economy of the household. Only a community of tough conservative habit can master it.[1]

Similarly, in Andrew Lytle's classic agrarian essay, "The Hind Tit," the industrialist-progressive wears city clothes. Lytle argues in his typically colorful form that industrial farming destroys the farm; Southern farmers shouldn't listen to the false prophets from the city:

---

1. Louis Rubin, Jr., *I'll Take My Stand: The South and the Agrarian Tradition* (Baton Rouge: Louisiana State Univ. Press, 1977), 15–16.

He must close his ears to these heresies that accumulate about his head, for they roll from the tongues of false prophets. He should know that prophets do not come from the cities, promising riches and store clothes. They have always come from the wilderness, stinking of goats and running with lice and telling of a different sort of treasure, one a corporation head would not understand. Until such a one comes, it is best for him to keep his ancient ways and leave the homilies of the tumble-bellied prophets to the city man.[2]

From a different but similar tradition, call it leftist agrarianism, Jacques Ellul paints the city quite strikingly:

The first undeniable element in this life is due to the city's nature as a parasite. She absolutely cannot live in and by herself. And this, moreover, characterizes all of those works of man by which he seeks autonomy. Everything takes its life from somewhere else, sucks it up. Like a vampire, it preys on the true living creation, alive in its connection with the Creator. The city is dead, made of dead things for dead people. She can herself neither produce nor maintain anything whatever. Anything living must come from outside. In the case of food, this is clear. But in the case of men also. We can't repeat too often that the city is an enormous man-eater. She does not renew herself from within, but by a constant supply of fresh blood from outside."[3]

Many of these suspicions about the city find sympathetic echoes in Scripture itself. These have not been lost on agrarian thinkers.

2. Ibid., 206.
3. Jacques Ellul, *The Meaning of the City* (Grand Rapids: Eerdmans Publ. Co., 1970), 150.

Doubts about the propriety of the city do find an interesting place in Scripture. Consider the long line of cursed city builders in contrast to Israel's nomadic shepherding. Cain was the first city builder. We learn that "Cain went out from the presence of the Lord and dwelt in the land of Nod, on the east of Eden" (Gen. 4:16). What did he do there? "And he built a city" (4:17).

In Noah's time, strong generational wickedness flowed through Ham, whose grandson Nimrod—"a mighty one on the earth"—was also dedicated to building cities:

> The beginning of his kingdom was Babel, and Erech, and Accad, and Calneh, in the land of Shinar. Out of that land went forth Asshur, and builded Nineveh, and the city Rehoboth, and Calah, And Resen between Nineveh and Calah: the same is a great city. (Gen. 10:10–12)

Nimrod started Babel, but his descendants most famously express the motives behind city building: "let us build us a city and a tower, whose top may reach unto heaven; and let us make us a name, lest we be scattered abroad upon the face of the whole earth.'" (Gen. 11:4). *They sought to make a name for themselves,* that's central, and they chose to display this attitude by constructing a city. Herein lies the basis of a theological suspicion against the city. To this day, city's motive and structure repeat those of ancient Babel.

That other model of ancient slavery, Egypt, continues this pagan affection for cities, when Pharaoh seeks to rein in the Israelites:

> Let us deal wisely with them; lest they multiply, and it come to pass, that, when there falleth out any war, they join also unto our enemies, and fight against us, and so get them up out of the land. Therefore they did set over them taskmasters to afflict them with their burdens. And they built for Pharaoh treasure cities. (Exod. 1:10–11)

As Israel progresses through Canaan, the city remains a constant obstacle, and, in reminiscence of Sodom, God destroys Jericho and thereafter directs his people against numerous pagan cities—'Israel vowed a vow unto the Lord, and said, 'If thou wilt indeed deliver this people into my hand, then I will utterly destroy their cities'" (Num. 21:2).

Like most Israelites, David was a country boy, a good shepherd. But as his son, Solomon, began to fall into more sin, he took a new delight in "storage cities" and "cities for his chariots, and cities for his horsemen" (1 Kgs. 9:19). Further in this descent, Rehoboam too finds need to build cities. He "dwelt in Jerusalem, and built cities for defense in Judah. . . . And in every city he put shields and spears, and made them exceeding strong, having Judah and Benjamin on his side" (2 Chr. 11:5,12). But alongside his devotion to city building, we find, "And it came to pass, when Rehoboam had established the kingdom and had strengthened himself, that he forsook the law of the Lord, and all Israel with him" (2 Chr. 12:1). Through Daniel we hear the ancient echoes of Babel when Nebuchadnezzar observes, "Is not this great Babylon, that I have built for the house of the kingdom by the might of my power, and for the honour of my majesty?" (Dan. 4:30).

This developing polemic against the city goes on and on, but, in thinking about such passages, passages of a contrary sort start crowding in. Scripture also portrays the city as a goal, a place of holiness, and this doesn't fit so nicely into a purely agrarian framework. The law not only promises Israel cities as a blessing (Deut. 19:7), the poets and prophets hold out the city as positive place: "For God will save Zion, and will build the cities of Judah: that they may dwell there, and have it in possession" (Ps. 69:35). Psalm 48 exalts in the truth, "Great is the Lord, and greatly to be praised in the city of our God, in the mountain of his holiness. Beautiful for situation, the joy of the whole earth, is mount Zion, on the sides of the north, the city of the great King" (48:1–2). Psalm 72 promises that as Messiah's kingdom comes, *cities* will prosper, "There shall be an handful of corn in the earth upon the top of the mountains; the fruit thereof shall shake like Lebanon: and they of the city shall flourish like grass of the earth" (72:16).

In one of the most delightful pictures of the spread of godliness through the reign of Messiah, Zechariah prophesies,

> Thus says the Lord: "I will return to Zion, And dwell in the midst of Jerusalem. Jerusalem shall be called the City of Truth, The Mountain of the Lord of hosts, The Holy Mountain." Thus says the Lord of hosts: "Old men and old women shall again sit in the streets of Jerusalem, Each one with his staff in his hand Because of great age. The streets of the city shall be full of boys and girls playing in its streets." (Zech. 8:3–5)

In similar fashion, both Ezekiel and, of course, the Book of Revelation picture the culmination of the people of God and all history in the image of a glorious city:

> And he carried me away in the spirit to a great and high mountain, and showed me that great city, the holy Jerusalem, descending out of heaven from God, having the glory of God: and her light was like unto a stone most precious, even like a jasper stone, clear as crystal; and had a wall great and high, and had twelve gates, and at the gates twelve angels, and names written thereon, which are the names of the twelve tribes of the children of Israel: on the east three gates; on the north three gates; on the south three gates; and on the west three gates. And the wall of the city had twelve foundations, and in them the names of the twelve apostles of the Lamb. And he that talked with me had a golden reed to measure the city, and the gates thereof, and the wall thereof. (Rev. 21:10–15)

So right alongside the pattern emphasizing the wicked origins of the city, we can find the contrary. In the end, the path from Genesis to Revelation is the path from garden to city. This is quite significant. Even Ellul notices that

> this is remarkable, because no other religion has so severely condemned the origins of civilization and man's civilizing acts and industrial progress—not to mention its specific attitude toward the city—as does the Judeo-Christian. Nevertheless, it is the city, death's domain, which appears as the crowning moment of history.[4]

Ellul just brushes this aside, but the scriptural affection for some form of city, even if purely symbolic, weakens the strong antithesis drawn by some forms of agrarian thinking.

What this shows us is that pure agrarianism—an agrarianism which includes in its essence a deep antipathy to the city—draws the cultural antithesis in a way different from Scripture. Christianity doesn't see the ultimate division standing between city and country but between the people and enemies of God, whether they dwell in skyscrapers or wheat fields. God's promises cut much more subtly than the mere difference between city and country: "if thou shalt hearken diligently unto the voice of the Lord thy God, to observe and to do all his commandments which I command thee this day, that the Lord thy God will set thee on high above all nations of the earth: And all these blessings shall come on thee, and overtake thee, if thou shalt hearken unto the voice of the Lord thy God. Blessed shalt thou be in the city, and blessed shalt thou be in the field" (Deut. 28:1–3). Divine blessing showers *both* the country and the city. Christianity can't be forced down the purely agrarian route.

Yet, something powerful still lingers from agrarian and biblical suspicions about the city. Who can deny the power of

4. Ibid., 162.

city or country life to mold us in certain directions, to shape our personalities? Even apart from those who know these truths by personal experience, several millennia of literature proves the truth that city people are very different from country people. If these differences had no connection to the respective environments at all, then we should regularly find city temperaments in the country and vice versa. But we don't. The two locations are not equal. The differences are tightly roped to their locations. Freeways and prairies can and do shape our deep loyalties, dictate our background values—those sheer curtains fluttering on our peripheral vision which set the whole mood of the room. It is here—in communal wisdom—where agrarianism and Christianity meet.

But what examples of communal wisdom do we find at the intersection of Christianity and agrarianism? What features make some aspects of country life superior to city life? These have to be features that can faithfully follow biblical notions of antithesis; that is, in the end, they need to be community values that can appear in either location, city or country, though they certainly show up more easily in the country. I'll suggest four features to think about, but such examples can take off in many directions.

Natural Humility: It's easier to be arrogant in the city than in the country. In the city, you are surrounded by human designs, human structures, human services. Everything is made by man for man. With little more than a twist or a flick, water flows, temperatures are regulated, heights are scaled, distances shortened, wounds healed, and square food sits patiently on laminated shelves waiting for its hunter. Needs are met without much sweat. Escape from snow, rain, heat, and wind is always a few steps away. The city is a grand blanket, insulating its people from the harshest elements, forcing back the sea and sky and wilds. In and of themselves such things are great blessings, but to the unreflective, such constant insulation encourages fables of self-sufficiency. We start to believe that man can do it all through wires and smarts.

But in the country you have to stand face to face with creation. It's not so easy to hide from the power of God. Nothing can stay the hand of dark blizzards or jagged blades of lightning. Rivers overflow their bounds like avalanches, and searing heat bleeds the strongest crops, and all you can do is pray and plead. And then you start all over again as the seasons change, bringing different faces of God. Wars cease, but the rotation of seasons doesn't—"Seedtime and harvest, cold and heat, winter and summer, and day and night shall not cease" (Gen. 8:22). The rhythms of God aren't insulated out of our lives.

Being face to face with God's handiwork humbles not only by terror but by beauty. In the country, you don't have thirty stories of concrete blocking His beauty. You see it every day when you lift your head. His art fills your eyes, demanding a bowed knee. His perfume and music cast their spells of His glory. And then you start the next day—living a life just beginning to grasp the Psalmist, "Day unto day utters speech, and night unto night reveals knowledge" (Ps. 19:2). The country reminds you daily of your place and what you are not.

Silent Markets: It's easier to know the importance of silence and peace in the country than in the city. A rebellious city is not a place of peace, of Sabbath. It is in constant movement, unending work. It rejects the rhythms and seasons of God and imposes its own exhausting drone and sleepless flow of electricity and wheels. It has no place for silence. Silence is terrifying; it reveals our bitter sin. The rebellious demand constant background noise as a shield against God.

It provides diversion from their souls, from the good life. Pascal noted that,

> Take away their distractions and you will see them wither from boredom. They feel their hollowness without understanding it, because it is indeed depressing to be in a state of unbearable sadness as soon as you are reduced to contemplating yourself. . . . That is why we like noise and activity so much. That is why imprisonment is such a horrific punishment. That is why the pleasure of being alone is incomprehensible.[5]

The modern city's most intrusive diversion is the omnipresent marketplace. It knows no limits. It intrudes upon every recreation, every work, every wall, every page, every quiet space. We allow the market to interrupt our stories and our meals. We use it to decorate our towns and our children. It is so pervasive that we fail to see its intrusiveness anymore, like an engine rattle or bad wallpaper. If we replaced every expression of the marketplace with a sign of the Church or State, people would scream tyranny.

If a truly unfettered market could ever rear its head in the modern world, it would certainly be a great blessing. Buying and selling are important parts of life—"She considereth a field, and buyeth it: with the fruit of her hands she planteth a vineyard" (Prov. 31:16). The evil is not in the marketplace but in our desires. We dictate what the market does. And we moderns insist that the marketplace intrude upon every corner of our lives. We have rejected the wisdom that there is "a time to keep silence" (Eccl. 3:7). A healthy Christian community, though, could quite easily recognize the place

---

5. Blaise Pascal, *Pensees and Other Writings*, trans. Honor Levi (New York: Oxford University Press, 1995), 16, 44 (§70 and §168, respectively).

of the market but deny it the power to suffocate every other sphere of life.

The city is designed for noise, but silence abounds in the mountains and prairies. One doesn't have to seek it in the country. It's given up quite easily. In fact, country silence can be quite frightening to city visitors. And such country silence long played an important part in medieval thinking, especially in the monastic spiritual disciplines. The best parts of medieval monastic life were an intriguing display of many Christian agrarian virtues. Quite apart from the monastic devotion to community living and quality vineyards, they understood the importance of silence.

In the section "On the Spirit of Silence," St. Benedict's Rule teaches, "since the spirit of silence is so important, permission to speak should rarely be granted even to perfect disciples, even though it be for good, holy edifying conversation; for it is written, 'In much speaking you will not escape sin' (Prov. 10:19), and in another place, 'Death and life are in the power of the tongue' (Prov. 18:21)." Sadly, the Rule also rejects "words that move to laughter, these we condemn everywhere with a perpetual ban." The correctives of the Reformation let the laughter break out once again. Yet still, even that Puritan of pleasure, Jonathan Edwards, could recognize that,

> A true Christian doubtless delights in religious fellowship and Christian conversation, and finds much to affect his heart in it; but he also delights in times to retire from all mankind, to converse with God in solitude. True religion disposes persons to be much alone in solitary places for holy meditation and prayer.[6]

6. Jonathan Edwards, *The Works of Jonathan Edwards*, vol. 1, Edward Hickman, ed. (Edinburgh: Banner of Truth, 1974 [1834]), 311–312.

The country is conducive to this aspect of the good life. It's hard to retire to solitude surrounded by pistons, off-ramps, and neon. Speed kills the soul.

Satisfying Labor: The country is also known for its difficult but satisfying labor, whereas the modern city is known for its tedious office and factory labor. There has to be some truth in the old Marxist complaint about factory life, no matter how much we as good Protestants want to talk about the priesthood of all occupations. Reality notifies us otherwise. All morally legitimate work may have dignity, but it's simply head-burying to assert that it's all equally satisfying and enjoyable. Stamping out the same metal part hour after hour or filling out eternal bureaucratic forms can't be as enjoyable as more creative occupations. Why kid ourselves? Solomon was honest enough about labor: "Therefore I hated life; because the work that is wrought under the sun is grievous unto me: for all is vanity and vexation of spirit. Yea, I hated all my labour which I had taken under the sun: because I should leave it unto the man that shall be after me" (Eccl. 2:17–18). Though we may be grateful that someone does the tedious work without complaining, would any parent really wish that upon his child? That's a sure test. Surely part of tedious labor is an added curse: "For God giveth to a man that is good in his sight wisdom, and knowledge, and joy: but to the sinner he giveth travail, to gather and to heap up, that he may give to him that is good before God. This also is vanity and vexation of spirit" (Eccl. 2:26). God says He gives tediousness to sinners. That should give us pause. Tedious labor isn't a romantic ideal. And yet, "the sleep of a laboring man is sweet, whether he eats little or much" (Eccl. 5:12). So Solomon recognizes a difference between the sweetness of labor and the tedious curse of "collecting and gathering" work.

Creativity makes part of the difference between laboring and mere gathering. We are made in the image of God, and we reflect that perhaps most clearly in our creativity. At creation, God was pleased with the creativity He brought to completion. Industrial labor often severs us from the completed work of our hands. We don't oversee the project from beginning to end; most tend to know only parts. Again, that's not sinful at all, but it has to be less than satisfying to never be able to mold something from beginning to end. That's why moderns have to have hobbies. They can't find satisfaction in their money-earning work, so many seek creative satisfaction in model planes and trains.

Compare industrial tediousness, though, with gardening and cooking. These activities, when done with even minimal love, allow a person to create from beginning to end. The gardener or farmer enlivens soil, plants a crop, battles weeds, submits to weather, tends to growth, and finally harvests a miracle. Of course, this sort of overseeing productivity can and does happen in the city, but it's not common in big industry. Bakers, woodcrafters, and plumbers can know it, but few industrial occupations do. And yet the middlemen and salesmen will always be with us, and still "he should make his soul enjoy good in his labour. This also I saw, that it was from the hand of God" (Eccl. 2:24). But this takes concerted effort. Tedious, assembly line work encourages bitterness. Being a part within a part of a corporate effort in satisfying unfaced masses can't help to begin to feel petty and insignificant in a way that midwifing carrots, corn, and tomatoes into the world never does.

Enjoying Personality: The city is notorious for its impersonality. Thousands of humans press past each other, thousands of fascinating stories to tell, and yet each is a stranger to the other. There isn't time to know the masses. The city has to distinguish people by affixing numbers to them, forced to overlook the intricacies of personality. Vast quantity isn't the only cause of impersonality though.

Quantity also has to breed distrust. Trust is the bond of community, and if we lack personal knowledge we can't trust. Without trust, our neighbors become constant threats of some sort. The modern city is simply too dangerous for familiarity. It demands distrust and protective aloofness to survive. Its people simultaneously complain about loneliness and yet desire anonymity.

Quantity not only breeds impersonality and distrust, it forces the city to place people into convenient types and categories. Since there is no time to know individuals, it's most convenient to throw out the distinguishing marks and lob everyone into general categories—black, Latino, Asian, white. It is no surprise that race conflict finds its origins in the city. It is the natural culmination of mass impersonality and distrust. The early Southern states get the slander for notorious racism (which later became a self-fulfilling prophecy), but before *the* war, the Northern cities were far harsher to black Americans. Of those pre-war years, Alexis de Toqueville noted of the North that,

> In that part of the Union where the Negroes are no longer slaves, have they become closer to the whites? Everyone who has lived in the United States will have noticed just the opposite. Race prejudice seems stronger in those states that have abolished slavery than in those where it still exists, and nowhere is it more intolerant than in those states where slavery was never known.[7]

7. Alexis de Toqueville, *Democracy in America,* vol. 1, 10, trans. G. Lawrence; ed. J. Mayer (New York: Harper and Row, 1988 [1848]), 343.

Even with slavery and the sins of the age, the South had a much more familial understanding of race. Again de Toqueville noted,

> In the South, where slavery still exists, less trouble is taken to keep the Negro apart: they sometimes share the labors and the pleasures of the white men; people are prepared to mix with them to some extent; legislation is more harsh against them, but customs are more tolerant and gentle.[8]

For the most part, even the more personal relation between the races has all but vanished in the modern South. They have come to ape city racial categories, rejecting the older appreciation for personality.

God has filled the earth with bizarre people, each one of us in his own way. One of the delights of poetry and storytelling is to see their mirror-work, the way they observe and catalogue our oddnesses and self-deceptions in such an intriguing manner. The human heart. Who can know it? Even in the dullest of us it bears onion layers of character. And all together we present such an intriguing diversity that "multiculturalists" haven't even begun to recognize. Such relativists are only concerned with abstract people; they hate real people.

Agrarian culture is well-known for its storytelling and love of personality. The city often tries the same, but it's not part of its soul. Small country towns get ridiculed for much, but they certainly burst with personality. This appreciation for personality finds a deeper foundation in Scripture itself. The parts of the body are important. They make up the life of the whole. Paul tells us,

> If the foot shall say, Because I am not the hand, I am not of the body; is it therefore not of the body? And if the ear

8. Ibid.

> shall say, Because I am not the eye, I am not of the body;
> is it therefore not of the body? If the whole body were an
> eye, where were the hearing? If the whole were hearing,
> where were the smelling? (1 Cor. 12:14–17)

This should constantly be before our minds as we think about Christian community. When it's prominent, we find a humble love and appreciation not only for our respective roles but also for our personality quirks. A healthy community has to not only tolerate personality differences but also enjoy them. We need all brands to make an intriguing, colorful community. And we need to know individual persons, not just city types. If we can do this, we'll find the reverse of the city trend. From love of personality, we'll see a natural flow of trust, and from trust, we'll get deep community. But we're all too far from this goal at this point.

A biblical view of bodily interdependence will also strongly curb some contemporary agrarian rhetoric. We sometimes hear agrarian calls for self-supporting farming and cultural independence which sounds curiously city-like. The city boasts of its self-sufficiency, and some agrarians end up doing the same thing on a single farm. Independency is not a Christian virtue, interdependency is. Andrew Lytle rejoices in this almost city self-sufficiency:

> Any man who grows his own food, kills his own meat,
> takes wool from his lambs and cotton from his stalks and
> makes them into clothes, plants corn and hay for his stock,
> shoes them at the crossroads blacksmith shop, draws milk
> and butter from his cows, eggs from his pullets, water
> from the ground, and fuel from the woodlot, can live in
> an industrial world without a lot of cash.[9]

9. Rubin, *I'll Take My Stand*, 244.

Though some truth lurks here, this doesn't fit with the picture of the community as body given by the Apostle Paul. The pure agrarian picture has one part doing everything, the eye playing the part of the hand, foot, and nose. The truth is that if we each attempted to do all of the above, then there could be no Andrew Lytles, no literature, for we would all be doing too much else. An interdependent community doesn't have to force everyone into the farmer's mold. It gives space to the doctor and theologian and poet.

Natural humility, silent markets, satisfying labor, enjoyment of personality—these are some of the bare necessities of a healthy community. They lie at the heart of Christian community and draw both from the wisdom of the country and of the city. All such communal wisdom is far more powerful than any location. It has to transcend location. In other words, if it is wisdom, we should be able to live and enjoy agrarian virtues in the city. Perhaps the best vision of such a community is the medieval town. There you avoid the radical self-sufficiency of the city and the purist agrarians, yet you also avoid the suffocating insulation from nature, dominating markets, and impersonality of the modern city.

Christian hope tells us that we can cultivate such a Christian community. But it won't be easy. The pessimists have already given up. Communities are grown, not constructed. It takes a self-conscious effort beginning in the family and the pulpit. Ortega Gasset noted that "the simple process of preserving our present civilization is supremely complex, and demands incalculably subtle powers." Amen. Our hope, though, is grounded not in our own powers but in the Spirit who can bless us "in the city, and . . . in the country" (Deut. 28:1, 3). For us, though, the faithful city of the future will resemble the country far more than it does any modern city.

CHAPTER 13

AND BABYLONS FALL

> Justice being taken away, then, what are kingdoms but great robberies? For what are robberies themselves, but little kingdoms? . . . Indeed, that was an apt and true reply which was given to Alexander the Great by a pirate who had been seized. For when that king had asked the man what he meant by keeping hostile possession of the sea, he answered with bold pride, "What thou meanest by seizing the whole earth; but because I do it with a petty ship, I am called a robber, whilst thou who does it with a great fleet art styled emperor."
>
> —Augustine, *City of God*

The long journey of medieval political thinking is one of the grandest stories of Christian antithesis, a fascinating tale of the conflict between pagan and Christian views of civil government. With short horizons, we might just as well say it was largely Augustine's doing, Augustine the African. A. N. Whitehead said that the whole history of philosophy is really just a footnote to Plato. Yet Augustine's influence on the West easily supersedes Plato's, touching not only philosophy but the broadest questions of culture. Even today, when debates arise over church-state relations, history, soteriology, creation, human nature, language, education, social progress, ecclesiology, Augustine is always loitering in the background, for good or ill. Yet Augustine himself wouldn't seek such credit. He would see himself as merely a conduit of biblical themes much more ancient than his efforts.

In the famous quote of Augustine above—a quote which deserves much more fame—there lurks the most important medieval questions about the nature of the State (to use a modern term). How does the State differ from a petty thief? Is it legitimate or illegitimate? If legitimate, what are its limits? What is justice? And is the justice something natural or supernatural? Is it inferior to the Church?

The contemporary medieval historian Norman Cantor, despite a typical Enlightenment nearsightedness in his treatment of Christianity, notes that at the turn of the first millennium, medieval political theory, grounded in Augustine, brought about "the first of the great world revolutions of western history,"[1] namely, the toppling of the State from its place of supremacy. But to truly appreciate this Christian contribution, we need to remember the centrality of the State in ancient pagan thinking.

In the ancient world, the State didn't just act like a god; they believed it was a manifestation of god. The State provided the connecting point between heaven and earth, and the ruler was not just a representative of a god, but most often he claimed divine attributes or even deity itself. This was true of the big boys like Egypt, Babylon, and Rome, but also of the countless animistic tribes whose supreme chiefs invaded medieval Europe. Whereas in biblical faith, God Himself oversees and directs all that comes to pass, in the pagan mind the world is largely chaos and the State provides

---

1. Norman Cantor, *The Civilization of the Middle Ages* (San Francisco: HarperPerennial, 1993), 244.

a very visible means of curtailing the fear of loose ends. It provides security in a wild world, and the modern welfare State makes the same promises. We may be most familiar with the claims to deity of the Roman emperors, such as the common references to Claudius as "our god Caesar" and the order to have a statue of Zeus made with Caligula's features. But this was in no way unique to Rome. Paganism commonly deified the State.

And the Son of God descended into the midst of this deeply rooted statism. This central event, this humble Incarnation and subsequent triumph, took captivity captive and imprisoned the slavery of pagan spiritual powers in the world—"having spoiled principalities and powers, he made a show of them openly, triumphing over them in it" (Col. 1:15). The enduring challenge to all Statisms, whether spiritual or secular, is the fact that the Father then, "raised him from the dead, and set him at his own right hand in the heavenly places, far above all principality, and power, and might, and dominion, and every name that is named, not only in this world, but also in that which is to come" (Eph. 1:20–22). Statists can't work with this. Whether ancient or modern, they treat the State as divine. It is the god who solves all problems and contains the chaos. The enemies of the early Christians recognized this conflict and complained, "and these are all acting contrary to the decrees of Caesar, saying there is another king, Jesus" (Acts 17:7). Christianity says, Yes; Christ is King over all authorities—including kings, emperors, dictators, and presidents. And so Christianity's first offenses were clearly political, and the situation hasn't changed.

The Christian medieval political revolution was the beginning of the outworking of these claims. The pagan statists wanted to continue the ancient tradition of making everything subordinated to the State, and the Christians balked at such treason to Christ. The medieval pagan hordes, our savage grandfathers and grandmothers, carried along their natural statism as they invaded medieval Europe. We have to remember that the paganism of European ancestors was so deep and brutal that they were still sacrificing humans for fun and profit up to the turn of the millennium. Their brutality and backwardness and cultural inferiority make contemporary African and South American tribes look like Rotary Clubs. It should be much easier for the Gospel to win modern tribes.

The central conflict focused upon the opposing claims of Church and State. The modern fable that the Enlightenment discovered the separation of Church and State is pure plagiarism. It plays upon our ignorance of medievalism. The separation of Church and State is a distinctively medieval, Christian, Hebraic contribution to world culture (yet Eastern Christianity always retained some pagan remnants of the divinity of both Church and State). The Hebraic influence is found in the separation of Church and State in the Old Testament through such events as King Uzziah's usurpation (2 Chr. 26:18). Of course, no medievalist embraced the Enlightenment fiction of neutrality in which separation of Church and State means separation of State from morality.

Though present in most of the early fathers, Augustine deservedly gets the most attention for setting the terms of the debate in terms of two independent institutions—the State as the expression of the City of Man and the Church as the expression of the City of God, the latter in keeping with the image at the close of the book of Revelation. Augustine explained that the Church will outlast all political kingdoms; She has divine promises. The State is usually just a robber, but at its best it can only keep the peace. It has no promises or grace to improve the people or morality. It can serve as a protector of the Church, who answers directly to Christ the King. Thus, the "Protestant" idea of sphere sovereignty, of the separation of Church and State, forged the medieval path quite early.

Gelasius I, bishop of Rome in the late fourth century, exposited this line of thought farther and more practically than Augustine. Whereas Augustine contended for the clear separation of Church and State, Gelasius argued that the Church was *auctoritas* and the State *potestas*. The Church defined morality, and the State could merely execute these definitions in its own temporal sphere; it lacked legislative authority. The move was clear. Legislative authority was generally held as supreme, and so the institutions were separate, with the Church being superior. This political Augustinianism held the day for centuries, during some of the greatest moments in the Church (though always far from perfection).

The older statism, however, kept rearing its head, especially after the turn of the millennium, interestingly on the heels of the second wave of pagan migrations. In the late medieval period, political Augustinianism expressed itself most clearly in the investiture controversies which appeared in several kingdoms. At its heart, the investiture disputes were Church-State disputes specifically concerned with whether civil authorities (kings and lords) had the authority to appoint church officers.

Through the eleventh century, the Gregorian reformers—the likes of Damiani, Humbert, Hildebrand—argued for the freedom of the Church from lay and civil intrusions. The struggle was bitter and prolonged and mixed in with the broader attempt to reform the Church, specifically with regard to ecclesiastical wealth, clerical morality, and authority. It was a movement which simultaneously expanded and undermined Church power, the former by reviving political Augustinianism, the latter by a devotion to poverty. The defining moment of the investiture controversy under the Gregorian reformer popes was the heated and subversive struggle between the Germanic Henry IV and Gregory VII (Hildebrand) in which the reckless emperor was finally forced to bow in repentance for violating the new stricter laws separating Church and State.

The ideas of political Augustinianism remained powerful, though the subsequent centuries saw greater and greater corruption of Church authority. Long gone were the Gregorian popes devoted to poverty. Extravagance and vice again won out. And in such circumstances, the elegance of the Augustinian-Gelasian doctrine turned into the curse of papal tyranny as the Church used its newly won supremacy to take on more and more explicitly civil functions. Yet the old, purer Augustinianism remained, permeating numerous reform and heretical movements, finally finding a fuller expression in the Protestant Reformation. There the likes of Calvin, the Huguenots, the Dutch Calvinists, the Covenanters, and the Puritans revived the earlier political Augustinianism, though much more thoroughly demarcated and thought out than at any other point in its development. We can find simple statements of it, for example, in the earliest Westminster Confession of Faith:

> The civil magistrate may not assume to himself the administration of the word and sacraments, or the power of the keys of the kingdom of heaven: yet he hath authority, and it is his duty to take order, that unity and peace be preserved in the church.
>
> . . . .
>
> Unto [the] visible catholic church Christ hath given the ministry, oracles, and ordinances of God, for the gathering and perfecting of the saints in this life, to the end of

the world; and doth by his own presence and Spirit, according to his promise, make them effectual thereunto.[2]

All the medieval elements are here: minimal state functions, servanthood of the State, the promised perseverance of the Church, prohibitions on State intrusions, and the distinctive, yet universal calling of the Church. Yet, even at that, the Protestant vision was far closer to the medieval mind than the modern. The same confession allowed kings to call synods and to suppress blasphemy, something we are forbidden even to think about in modernity. The Protestants were far more medieval than Rome. The Protestants not only sought out the fathers, especially Augustine, for the truth of salvation, they revived early political thinking, developing it further into discussions of liberty, tyranny, elections, state limits, and freedom of conscience long since secularized and bled white by moderns.

In comparison to both modern and ancient paganism, Christianity stands out as decidedly anti-statist. The State is not the hope of the world; it is an institution grounded in the threat of violence, whether via capital punishments or petty bureaucratic intrusions. Behind this Christian anti-Statism we can't help but hear the scriptural threats about the nature of the State in that classic and tragic passage where rebellious Israel demanded a king:

> Now make us a king to judge us like all the nations. But the thing displeased Samuel, when they said, Give us a king to judge us. And Samuel prayed unto the Lord. And the LORD said unto Samuel, Hearken unto the voice of the people in all that they say unto thee: for they have not rejected thee, but they have rejected me, that I should not reign over them. (1 Sam. 8:6–7)

2. *Westminster Confession of Faith*, XXIII.3 and XXV.3.

The passage goes on to itemize many of the curses that a king brings with him—taxation, conscription, war, property violations, and more, all the conveniences of the modern State. If you look at the passage you see that the promised tyranny to Israel at that time was far less than any modern nation. The response is not to dream about revolution or childish tax resistance. The curse of the State is from God's own hand. Lasting liberty can only come through repentance.

But the passage shouldn't just make us think about the gross tyrannies of our time. The truth is that at base even a nontyrannical king or president is a sign of our collective lack of self-control. The existence of civil authorities should always be a reminder that we are so immature as a people that we cannot live our lives peacefully on our own in submission to the divine commands. Every kingly, presidential, or prime ministerial seal should bear the inscription: "They have not rejected thee; but they have rejected Me, that I should not reign over them" (1 Sam. 8:7). There have been godly kings, kings with whom God has been pleased, contrary to Anabaptistic claims. Yet the goal should be "no king but Christ."

The opening quote from Augustine contained not only the seeds of his more elaborate Church-State doctrine but also questions about the nature of civil justice. One of the most enjoyable parts of medieval Christianity is that it wasn't embarrassed by Christ. They believed it all, and then some. That's so refreshing. It's hard today to find Christians of any stripe, but especially Protestant leaders, who aren't embarrassed by some aspect of the Scriptural message.

We have swallowed whole all the Enlightenment "religion-horror-stories" that it is supposed to hurt us to think about any time prior to the New Deal. Yet even the ugliness of much of medieval political life pales in comparison to the horrors of the French Revolution and most of the theft, butchery, nuclear threats, terrorism, and genocide of the twentieth century. And yet, the medieval period, for its relative peace and progress, gets the slanderous label—the Dark Ages, and the Age of Absolutism gets called the Enlightenment. From the victor come the titles.

Along these lines, Harold O. J. Brown notes that,

> The conversion of Constantine inaugurated Christian Europe. The civilization that subsequently developed is in disrepute now, for a variety of reasons. In my opinion, however, it compares favorably with pre-Christian paganism and with post-Christian degeneracy.
>
> American secular tradition sneers at Constantine, because he began the process of creating a Christian state. The American evangelical tradition disdains him, because he established *Catholicism* as the empire's official faith (a Catholicism not yet Roman, of course). . . . Americans speak with relief rather than regret of being post-Constantinian and sometimes of being post-Christian.[3]

In political talk, evangelicals are especially terrified by almost any hint of biblical law. Some actually think it is a recent and novel notion to reflect upon current questions in the light of biblical law. But to King David and many medieval kings, biblical law was one of the sweetest expressions of liberty on the face of the earth. While the pagans were prostituting marriage bonds and butchering their children, biblical law laid out clear protections for widows and orphans. One of the great Christian medieval kings, King Alfred of the Saxons, who ruled late in the ninth century, specified a

---

3. Harold O. J. Brown, "Introduction to Christian America" in Gary Scott Smith, *God and Politics* (Phillipsburg: Presbyterian and Reformed Publ., 1989), 130–131.

law code in which he inserted Mosaic commandments and explained,

> These are the dooms which the Almighty God Himself spake unto Moses, and commanded him to keep: and after the only begotten Son of the Lord, our God, that is, our Savior Christ, came on earth, He said that He came not to break nor to forbid these commandments, but with all good to increase them.[4]

Similarly King Canute's (A.D. 1016–1035) Danish/Saxon law code explained,

> The first provision is, that I desire that justice be promoted and every injustice zealously suppressed, that every illegality be rooted up and eradicated from this land with the utmost diligence, and the law of God promoted. And henceforth all men, both poor and rich shall be regarded as entitled to the benefit of the law, and just decisions shall be pronounced on their behalf.[5]

One of the most influential political theorists of the medieval period, and one from whom the Reformers drew, was John of Salisbury (A.D. 1115–1180) in his famous political treatise *Policraticus*. Much of the text is a running commentary on Old Testament political themes. At various places he upholds the Christian emphasis on having the prince, the State, constrained under the limits of law, specifically divine law. The prince is not above the law, a theme carried on strongly by the later Protestants.

> When he sits upon the throne of his kingdom, he will write for himself a copy of this law of Deuteronomy in a

---

4. Cited in Stephen Perks, *Christianity and Law* (Whitby: Avant Books, 1993), 64

5. Cited ibid., 28.

book. See that the prince must not be ignorant of law and, although he takes pleasure in many privileges, he is not permitted to be ignorant of the laws of God on the pretext of the martial spirit. . . . All censures of law are void if they do not bear the image of divine law; . . . Christian princes can be instructed by our Constantine, Theodosius, Justinian, and Leo and other most Christian princes. For in fact they gave particular effort in order that the most sacred laws, which bind the lives of all, should be known and upheld by all.[6]

In an era when "crimes" of inequality draw far more scandal than theft, adultery, or even murder, it is hard for moderns to appreciate the wisdom of biblical law. The Apostle James described Old Testament law as the "law of liberty" (Jas. 1:25). And King David declared, "And I will walk at liberty, for I seek thy precepts" (Ps. 119:45). Yet we moderns fail to recognize the deep connection between biblical commands and freedom. As others have noted, if a modern State were to embrace biblical law, the result would probably look more like the absence of a State than an Islamic tyranny or the "family values" of the Christian right (which of the two is more frightening?). We are far too immature to face the radical liberties of biblical law. We have such State-induced slave mentalities that we couldn't handle the responsibilities of real freedom. We'll have to leave that to future centuries.

But for all our misconceptions about biblical law, most Christians are just embarrassed by the thought of it. Yet if we completely set aside any idea of actually implementing biblical law in any contemporary setting (which in most cases, such an imposition itself would be a violation of biblical law), Christians have to consider what God Himself thinks of His

6. John of Salisbury, *Policraticus*, Cary Nederman, trans. and ed. (Cambridge: Cambridge Univ. Press, 1990), 41–42.

law. At the very start, God's prophet Moses seeks to "sell" the goodness of His commandments by showing how well they compare to the laws of the surrounding nations.

> Keep therefore and do them; for this is your wisdom and your understanding in the sight of the nations, which shall hear all these statutes, and say, "Surely this great nation is a wise and understanding people." For what nation is there so great, who hath God so nigh unto them, as the LORD our God is in all things that we call upon him for? And what nation is there so great, that hath statutes and judgments so righteous as all this law, which I set before you this day? (Deut. 4:6,8)

And all of King David's Psalm 119 is a chorus about the beauty and goodness of God's laws. It's hard to see how any Christian can read that Psalm and yet still refuse to acknowledge the superiority of the wisdom of God's commands.

> The law of thy mouth is better unto me than thousands of gold and silver. (v. 72)
> O how love I thy law! it is my meditation all the day. (v. 97)
> I have more understanding than all my teachers: for thy testimonies are my meditation. (v. 99)
> I understand more than the ancients, because I keep thy precepts. (v. 100)
> How sweet are thy words unto my taste! yea, sweeter than honey to my mouth! (v. 103)
> Thy testimonies have I taken as an heritage for ever: for they are the rejoicing of my heart. (v. 111)
> Therefore I love thy commandments above gold; yea, above fine gold. (v. 127)

If David was so overpowered by the wisdom and wonders of God's law, how dare we belittle it? David's testimonies about God's law are a good test of our embarrassment. Can you confess their wisdom alongside David, the man after

God's own heart? Or has your tradition kept you from this joy? We should have Christ's confidence in regard to His law. He could say, "Whosoever therefore shall break one of these least commandments, and shall teach men so, he shall be called the least in the kingdom of heaven: but whosoever shall do and teach them, the same shall be called great in the kingdom of heaven" (Mt. 5:19).

The apostles, too, didn't associate biblical law with tyranny and legalism. They saw it as the summary expression or definition of godly love. The apostle John taught that, "This is love, that we walk after His commandments" (2 Jn. 1:6). In his previous letter, he makes the same point: "By this we know that we love the children of God, when we love God and keep His commandments. For this is the love of God, that we keep His commandments. And His commandments are not grievous" (1 Jn. 5:2–3). The Apostle Paul explicitly connects various Mosaic commands with love:

> Owe no man any thing, but to love one another: for he that loveth another hath fulfilled the law. For this, Thou shalt not commit adultery, Thou shalt not kill, Thou shalt not steal, Thou shalt not bear false witness, Thou shalt not covet; and if there be any other commandment, it is briefly comprehended in this saying, namely, Thou shalt love thy neighbour as thyself. Love worketh no ill to his neighbour: therefore love is the fulfilling of the law. (Rom. 13:9–10)

Love is the fulfillment of the law. We can think of the law not as a bureaucratic code but as a chest of wisdom, an elaborate answer to the question, what is love? And then we point to biblical law. That is why David can rejoice. Biblical law isn't tyranny; it is honey to the lips. Both Old and New covenants confirm this. If we could only get evangelicals to do the same.

Despite all this honey and gold, one poor medieval option is resurfacing, namely, the hope of natural law, the desire for a natural and universal moral code. Some prominent natural law advocates want us to recognize an objective code of morality in nature, specifically human nature, that won't be offensive to non-Christians. Despite countless epistemological problems with this approach, one rarely mentioned Christian criticism of natural law is that it doesn't fit into a Christian view of reality. As noted in several places in this book, the medieval period was a protracted struggle between Christianity and paganism, especially Hellenistic paganism of Plato and Aristotle.

Natural law theory stems originally from this Greek view of reality. The Aristotelians were especially prominent in the history of natural law thinking. In the Aristotelian worldview, invisible, eternal, objective norms make up the inner structure of everything on the earth. Everything has one of these mysterious essences lurking within, and these metaphysical norms determine the structure and function and goals of the object in question, including humans. Most natural law theorists have to assume such a view of reality to even begin their accounts.

Yet for Protestants to embrace Aristotle out of embarrassment for biblical law is quite a curious move. It quite blatantly invites us to embrace pagan categories of thought, thus violating all the commands of antithesis. Aristotelian forms were always a pagan substitute for the functions of the biblical God, i.e., creation, providence, omniscience, and holiness. With natural law, we lose both historical progress and antithesis. It seems much more faithful just to confess with David, "Oh, how I love Your law! It is my meditation all the day."

But natural law advocates do have a serious worry about connecting Christian culture to contemporary life. Non-Christians get terrified when Christians start talking about gaining political power and winning county seats. And from what most evangelicals find important enough to impose on their neighbors by threat of State, I worry too. We should all confess that modern Christians are too modern to be able to appreciate the wisdom of statecraft. We don't grasp necessary wisdom. Instead we lobby for prayer in government schools and try to ban Hollywood blasphemies and sing of vigilante murders of abortionists. We should want no part of this mere scraping at the edges.

The entire medieval and Protestant tradition is anti-Statist, and that includes, as Augustine taught us, the view that the State is the least important institution among Church, State, and Family. Yet, the great irony of the Christian Right is that though their families are often messes and their churches splintering, they think they have the wisdom to wield the sword. In search of "real change," they charge out to conquer the institution that is most impotent in actually bringing it about. We haven't changed much from our ancient Israelite brothers. We want a king or a sword just like everybody else. We don't understand how God has structured the world, how real change occurs.

The glitz of politics is a great deception. Power draws the pagan-hearted. But we so easily neglect Christ's teaching,

> But Jesus called them unto him, and said, Ye know that the princes of the Gentiles exercise dominion over them, and they that are great exercise authority upon them. But it shall not be so among you: but whosoever will be great among you, let him be your minister; And whosoever will be chief among you, let him be your servant. (Mt. 20:25–27)

Why should we want to wield any political party club or rule any council at this stage of life? The State is a superficial, testy institution that is merely a shifting symptom of deeper realities. And so a reformation of the State should be like healing a sore throat. Nurture the rest of the body with good things first, and the throat will follow along in time.

But such a rejection of contemporary political action is very different from rejecting Christian political theory. That would be a stifling of the Lordship of Christ. Christians have a grand tradition of political thought, raising insights often quietly sneaked away by less creative Enlightenment thinkers. We can meditate on political wisdom, while not neglecting the weightier matters of the law.

CHAPTER 14

RIGHTS OF DEGREE

HIERARCHY AND HUMILITY IN THE WORLD GOD MADE

O, when degree is shaked,
Which is the ladder of all high designs,
The enterprise is sick . . .
Take but degree away, untune that string
And hark what discord follows. Each thing meets
In mere oppugnancy . . .
Force should be right, or rather right and wrong . . .
Then everything include itself in power,
Power into will, will into appetite
And appetite, an universal wolf,
So doubly seconded with will and power,
Must perforce make an universal prey
And last eat up himself.

—William Shakespeare, *Troilus and Cressida*

The atmosphere in which modernity lives and moves is that of egalitarianism. Because of this, and because we have managed to believe our own lies about liberty, fraternity, and equality for so long, we tend to react to the medieval vision as irredeemably hierarchical. In this we are at least partly correct—the medieval world cannot be understood apart from hierarchy and cannot be separated from it. But as moderns, we have a fervent and religious belief in equality, and we believe with unquestioned strength that any denial of equality leads inexorably to all kinds of tyrannical abuses. So, before proceeding further, we should reflect on Ulysses' speech in *Troilus and Cressida* and attempt to see how the medieval mind would see the real alternatives.

Modernity only believes in the language of equality—we do not mind tyrannies as long as they are draped in the name of the people, all of whom must be *formally* acknowledged to be equal. The tyrant may actually be engaged in trying to murder all the people, but as long as he bows and scrapes in front of the Temple of Democracy, his position is secure. But in the medieval mindset, in the world God made, our only real choice is between glad and voluntary submission to natural authority on the one hand or forced submission to naked power on the other. The choice is *not* between evil submission and good equality. As C. S. Lewis comments, "The modern idea that we can choose between Hierarchy and equality is, for Shakespeare's Ulysses, mere moonshine. The real alternative is tyranny; if you will not have authority you will find yourself obeying brute force."[1]

The medieval approach was thoroughly comfortable with hierarchy and authority, and understood the differences between authority and power. A return to the medieval way of thinking necessitates a return to this understanding; an inescapable feature of medieval thinking is that it is hierarchical. There is no getting around it; the subject must simply be addressed. And we must address it with true sympathy, or there will be no return to a medieval vision. This must be emphasized because egalitarianism is so deeply embedded in the modern mind that thinking outside of egalitarian assumptions is extraordinarily difficult. Of all the assumptions

1. Lewis, *A Preface to Paradise Lost*, 75.

which characterize the medieval mind, the stand against egalitarianism is evidently the most unpopular and excites the most odium. Again Lewis: "[such] words, thus taken at their face value, are very startling to a modern audience; but those who cannot face such startling should not read old books."[2] This is not an old book, but it does reflect some older assumptions which require explanation, and we beg our readers' patience.

Not surprisingly, if this is the case, then at least some caveats must be stated at the outset. First, an assertion of hierarchy in no way sets aside the biblical requirements of humility, or the scriptural warnings about the insidiousness of pride. Rather, it postulates a world in which rank and station exist, and therefore it is necessary to recognize the importance of humility. "Let nothing be done through strife or vainglory; but in lowliness of mind let each esteem others better than themselves" (Phil. 2:3). Conditioned by egalitarianism the way we have been, we think that any assertion of hierarchy contains the clear diabolical desire to "be superior" to others, which is pride and arrogance. Certainly any such desire, considered by itself, is pride and arrogance. But we conveniently forget that our egalitarian zeal may be reflecting the same grasping attitude—an intense desire not to "be inferior" to anyone. All such problems are located in the heart, and not in the station to which God has assigned us. Granting this, it is still fair to say that the older aristocratic ideas of *noblesse oblige* were far closer to the biblical ideal than the sullen, sidelong glances we give people today in order to ensure that no one gets any more than we do. In the older view, men could and did reject the biblical standards in their attitudes. The standard was humility, although

2. Ibid., 76.

medieval sinners of course fell short of it in practice. But in the modern world, the standard itself has been corrupted. We have institutionalized insolent envy, and we believe we are advocates of justice when we are simply displaying our petulance.

Another preliminary point must also be made, in which we try to set aside the popular misconception of the medieval idea of authority. Modernists, who are ignorant of how a self-consciously hierarchical society could possibly function, think of any hierarchy in grossly simplistic terms. They assume that hierarchy means we must adopt the straightforward hegemony of Yertle the Turtle. Because the Middle Ages were comfortable with hierarchy, we simply assume that all medieval kings were oriental despots, and of course we all picture the pope at the top of the towering column that was medieval Europe. But the growth of papal authority (which many people wrongly identify with medievalism) was actually the single greatest harbinger of modernity. The evolution of the arbitrary absolutism in the papacy was the prototype of all the various Enlightenment absolutisms. The claim for *any* governmental ultimacy on earth is the heartbeat of secularist thinking. Initially, of course, it had to be done in the name of God, but later the same absolutism could be preached in the name of man.

Now the papacy in this form was of course resisted by the Reformers, but they were not the first ones. In this respect the Reformers were simply carrying on a grand medieval tradition, one which even included their ready identification of the pope as the antichrist. He would be a brave man who sought to maintain that Dante was not a man of the Middle Ages, or that *Piers Plowman* did not represent the medieval mindset. The conciliarists were also men of the Middle Ages, and when they resolved the papal schism of Rome and

Avignon, they were acting as typical men of their age. John Wyclif was a medieval priest, and the Archbishop of Canterbury Thomas Bradwardin had no patience with pilgrimages and meritmongers. Many falsely assume that the medieval Church was simply an unbroken Roman Catholicism, and then in the early sixteenth century the Reformers decided to veer off and do something entirely different. In this understanding the Reformation was the religious counterpart to the Renaissance, both of which marked the birth of the modern world.

The actual course of events was much different, and much more complex. One of the complexities is that throughout the medieval period, many anticipations of modernity were growing, and during the Reformation many aspects of medievalism were retrieved and restored. During the medieval period, many issues were thoroughly unsettled in the Church, and various claims and denials of papal supremacy were at the forefront of that list. One important objection to the papal claims of the Roman church is that it is a *modern* development. C. S. Lewis pointed to this tendency in his answer to one correspondent who asked why he was not a Roman Catholic. His reply was charitable, but profound in its implications from anyone as well-versed in the literature of the medieval period as Lewis was. "By the time I had really explained my objection to certain doctrines which differentiate you from us (and also in my opinion from the Apostolic *and even the Medieval Church*), you would like me less" (emphasis ours).[3]

Now with these qualifications made, it remains necessary to present the positive case for hierarchy to egalitarian

---

3. C. S. Lewis, *Letters of C. S. Lewis* (London: Harcourt Brace & Co., 1966), 406.

ears. Because hierarchy is usually thought to be synonymous with tyranny, this presents a slight difficulty. In such a situation, disclaimers concerning the Crusades and Inquisition are usually thought to be necessary, but this is actually one disclaimer which we do not need to make. The actual behavior of egalitarian modernists has managed to kill more innocent people in our century than 100,000 Grand Inquisitors combined could ever have done. The shame, embarrassment, and mortification should belong entirely to the secular modernists, to those who think that their pretensions of equality have ever led to anything other than a tyrannical denial of liberty and all the subsequent bloodbaths. The first victim on the altar of equality is always that of liberty. The second victim is a collective one, a long line of men, women, and children which stretches out of sight. Hearing modernists talk about the bloody abuses of the Middle Ages is like hearing a lecture on disease control by Typhoid Mary, and it is all a bit much.

But now *ad propositum*. The hierarchical nature of the universe is a given in the medieval framework. Lewis again: "According to this conception degrees of value are objectively present in the universe. Everything except God has some natural superior; everything except unformed matter has some natural inferior. The goodness, happiness, and dignity of every being consists in obeying its natural superior and ruling its natural inferiors."[4] Cork should float and lead shouldn't. Everything, *unless sin and discord has entered*, naturally and voluntarily seeks its appointed level. When lead wants to float, the lead has a sin problem. Because God has given us choices, we may sinfully choose to want something other than what He has given. Adults may want to be

4. Lewis, *A Preface to Paradise Lost*, 73.

children, or women may want to be men, or laboring men may want to be king. But the issue is whether or not God has blessed this desire through His configuration of the world. The modern child is told that he can be anything that he wants to be. The medieval child would have been instructed on how to occupy his station. A moment's reflection should tell us which child is being told the lie.

Discovering this station is not the result of long pro-tracted negotiations. Neither is it hammered out in a social contract. It is entirely voluntary, and it is the result of glad submission to how God made the world. In order that it may be protected, occupying one's station must not be bureaucrat-ically determined, and it must not be settled through some *a priori* restriction of "labor mobility." Liberty, of necessity, is anti-egalitarian. Calhoun once said that he loved liberty and hated equality. The two are linked, and the converse is also true. Anyone who hates equality, must love liberty. In the medieval conception, it is just as much a delight to find your natural superiors as it is to find those whom you should govern as your inferiors. But the words keep slapping us in the face. Inferior? Superior? *Who do they think they are?* The fact that we feel personally insulted is simply an indication of how thoroughly we have been propagandized. We know instinctively that the use of words such as these will neces-sarily do great damage, although none of us has seen such damage, and we all think the use of words like "equality" is perfectly safe although we have lived in a century in which equality has slain her millions. Lenin's category of useful idiots is probably larger than he could possibly have hoped.

Modernity defines ambition as the desire to get to the top, assuming that this is where everyone should want to be. If someone does not get there, he has a legitimate grievance against whoever held him back. Modernity thinks of our entire existence as a great footrace, which everyone should want to win. But the medievalist would define legitimate ambition as the desire to identify one's station and attempt to get there, regardless of the dignity of that station. The medievalist thinks of our entire existence as a dance, in which some bow and some curtsey, some play the music and some dance, some laugh in gladness and some try to flatter the ladies. The irony, the last being first and all that, is that when a man finds a lowly station in cheerful obedience, he acquires in this a great dignity. He knows what he is supposed to do in the dance, and he is happy to do it. In the medieval world, a simple stable hand could be content with his station. Today a union member glares at management, and calls it his moral duty.

Of course the first question to ask is whether this medieval understanding is scriptural. We must be careful because in one sense the evidence for a hierarchical view of society is everywhere throughout the Bible. We ignore the global evidence, take a few verses out of context, give them a little egalitarian spin, and think we are being scriptural. "There is neither Jew nor Greek, there is neither bond nor free, there is neither male nor female: for ye are all one in Christ Jesus" (Gal. 3:28). But Paul of course is talking about our justification and our standing before God. In this sense, all men are equal—we will all stand before the judgment seat of Christ, and on that great Day, sex, race, wealth, and so forth will not determine anything, for God does not show partiality. And in this sense, neither may we show partiality in our courts of law.

But such considerations, important to remember, do not give us the Bible's assumptions about societal relations. A land is blessed when the king is the son of *nobles* (Eccl. 10:17). When God established the throne of Solomon, He did so by granting him *majesty*. "And the Lord magnified Solomon exceedingly in the sight of all Israel, and bestowed upon him such royal majesty as had not been on any king before him in Israel" (1 Chr. 29:25). Solomon was not just one of the guys who happened to be in the right place at the right time. Solomon himself laments what happens when the degree is taken away. "Folly is set in great dignity, and the rich sit in a low place. I have seen servants upon horses, and princes walking as servants upon the earth" (Eccl. 10:6–7). What he has seen is appalling to him. The thing is not right. When wisdom speaks her mind, she says that a well-ordered aristocratic society depends upon how *she* bestows the harmony. "By me kings reign, and princes decree justice. By me princes rule, and nobles, even all the judges of the earth" (Prov. 8:15–16). A careful reading of Scripture shows that the biblical view of society has much more in common with the medieval conception than does our modern notion.

Everything is not uniform; we must distinguish two forms of dignity. The first is dignity of office, and the second we may describe as dignity of character. The first is illustrated by terms such as husband, or chief, or mother. The second is illustrated by phrases such as good man, brave leader, or kind woman. When the two dignities correspond, life is harmonious. When a man holds a superior office, but is an inferior man, then everything is out of joint. "Folly is set in great dignity, and the rich sit in a low place" (Eccl. 10:6).

This gives us perspective on how the medievalists would define the various offenses surrounding a lack of societal harmony. When a man seeks to rule his natural equals, or is willing to obey them, this is either tyranny on the one hand or servility on the other. If a man fails to obey a natural superior or neglects to rule a natural inferior, this is either rebellion or abdication respectively. Our duties extend in all directions. Because moderns think that authority is simply power, they do not know how to do anything but boss people around or chafe at being bossed, with the whole travesty sprinkled liberally with the rhetoric of equality.

It is significant that Ulysses describes the disordering of stations to the action of untuning a string. When we remember that one of the principal characteristics of the medieval world was its love of harmony, this should not surprise us. And if we learn that the principle characteristic of modernity is its societal discord, we should remain unsurprised.

CHAPTER 15

HERITAGE OF HARMONY

LOVING TOOLS WITHOUT IDOLATRY

In several places C. S. Lewis points to one of the great characteristics of the medieval mind, which was an immense capacity for systematic harmonization. The Middle Ages were bookish, and through the workings of providence the books medieval men had inherited were few, scattered, and representative of many diverse schools of thought. But because they had such a high respect for books, they sought to harmonize them all. "Faced with this self-contradictory corpus, they hardly ever decided that one of the authorities was simply right and the others wrong: never that all were wrong. To be sure, in the last resort it was taken for granted that the Christian writers must be right as against the Pagans. But it was hardly ever allowed to come to the last resort."[1] This desire for peace led to some absurdities, and we trust we may learn from medieval errors as well as medieval wisdom. But the purpose of making this observation is to bring their wisdom to bear on one of our principal difficulties—our uneasy relationship to technology.

Our tendency as moderns is to embrace dialectical absurdities. We harmonize nothing. We live in a fragmented

---

1. C. S. Lewis, *Studies in Medieval and Renaissance Literature* (London: Cambridge University Press, 1966), 45.

world, and progress is only the result of a blind struggle between colliding opposites. One characteristic of the modern mind is that at the first sign of any disagreement, we are willing to rush to the barricades and declare our undying animosity toward . . . whatever. In line with this, as the ugliness of modernity has become increasingly evident, many of modernity's sons have been heading for the mountains of Montana, resolved in their hearts to live close to the land. But such earth muffins, in reaction, far from standing against modernity, are simply one more manifestation of it. A back-to-the-land antithesis answers the skyscraper thesis, and the fragmented hostility continues. The Enlightenment experiment, with all its actions and reactions, may perhaps be described as several centuries on the Hegelian Tilt-a-Whirl.

But the medieval mind is interested in harmonizing as much as can be harmonized, and sometimes even a little more. When modernity was born, it came into existence breathing contempt for the "Middle Ages." The two were belligerents, and it appeared for some time that modernity had won that war. But after centuries of trying to navigate without a compass (having smashed all the old ones), modernity appears to be at least somewhat chastened and is looking around for alternatives.

The alternatives which present themselves are rarely true alternatives. Our problem is that *revolutions* against modernity are quintessentially . . . modern. And anything less than a revolution will only result in some new fad within the context of modernity, leading to nothing more than new ways of decorating our restaurants—postmodern retro, say. The modernist nature of our dilemma is illustrated by our tendency to equate conservatism with being "right-wing." But as the history of the phrase indicates, a right-winger is really only a modest revolutionary. After the French Revolution, the temperate revolutionaries sat on the right side of the legislative chamber while the fire-eaters sat on the left. But they were all revolutionaries. The right-wing is a revolutionary category within the confines of modernity. Indeed, the whole idea of political parties as such is a revolutionary idea. The right-wing really only has one set of options. On the one hand, it may quietly tag along behind the radicals, acquiescing in their role as slow revolutionaries. This is the "conservative" option scorned by R. L. Dabney as the mere shadow that follows radicalism to perdition. Or the right-wing may take drastic action and take up arms against the current foolishness. But if they do this successfully, when the smoke clears, we will find ourselves with a new set of despots, with perhaps a bit more sense on economic matters. Violent overthrow of the revolution is revolutionary, and compromise with the revolution is revolutionary. The medieval vision presents another way entirely—not the right-wing of recent memory, and not the radical right, but rather a conservatism of *temper,* one which is organically tied to the family, to the Church, and to the soil.

Our intent in this book is to present this medieval mentality as a genuine alternative to modernity, and not just another spasmodic reaction to it. This means that what we have inherited must be harmonized with what we want to develop, and what we have received are the fruits of modernity—both sweet and bitter. This harmonization must be done at a most profound level, and yet done slowly and cautiously. It must *really* be accomplished, and not with a view to finishing it *now*. In one sense, we are not calling upon the works of modernity to die, but rather to grow up. The process will take a century or so, which is perfectly fine. The medieval mind is patient. In the process, technology will continue to progress, but modernity is clearly dying.

We do not lament the continued development of technological ideas. We are not driven by a medieval nostalgia. Many mental pictures look quite fine from a distance, especially through a romantic haze, but a closer inspection reveals more than a few problems. For example, when we consider the nostalgic tendency to airbrush our images of the pre-industrial past, we should begin to suspect ourselves. A snow-covered cottage graces the front of a Christmas card quite well, but not indicated is the absence of indoor plumbing, adequate lighting, sanitary food storage, safety in child-bearing, and so on, *ad quitealonglistem*. A lot of this was changed when we staggered into the modern world, and there is no question that when it comes to various creature comforts, we are all doing very well, thank you. Three cheers for central heating, antibiotics, and all of that. Nevertheless, these considerable perks of modernity did have quite a price tag attached, and for many years agrarian thinkers— men like Weaver and Lytle—warned us about the payments pending. What does it profit a man if he gain the whole world, but lose his own soul? Against the iron demands of modernity, an agrarian and medieval vision calls us back to live close to the land, close to family, close to our *souls*. This has lured some in an anti-technology direction. But Luddite revolts which smash all the machinery are really nothing but employment opportunities for the repairmen. As seen earlier, modernist revolts against modernity do not address the problem, and end with the frustrated and defiant logic of the Unabomber.

Initially, despite the personal comforts, the logic of industrialization at the broader cultural level was all in the direction of macro-ugliness—urbanization, pollution, fast-lane mindlessness, and so forth. As one singer responded to it a number of years ago, "Don't it make you want to go home?"

For those who value more humane values, as we have presented them in this book, industrialization has usually been written off as an unmitigated bummer—a cultural cancer which has devoured the beautiful and destroyed the lovely. But a more optimistic view is possible; consider the organic possibility that industrialization was simply several centuries of cultural acne as we were working our way up through societal adolescence.

The medieval vision is coming back into its own, but not as a reactionary return to the *status quo ante*. Neither is it "right-wing" in any sense of the word. Rather, the agrarian revival is the next step after technopoly and is only possible because of certain successful results of industrialization. For example, the massive decentralization we see happening all around us is the child of the electronics revolution. This is not presented as agreement with the typical cyberhype—we do not think that the silicon chip can remove original sin. Nor do we think it can teach our children or write our books. But in the providence of God, the great pride of modernity, the centralized state, is going the way of the trilobite. In its idolatrous pride, industrialism mistook its own trajectory, and thought to fly forever. But in the emergence of a decentralized society, one *creature* is now replacing another creature. As we write this book at electronic keyboards, we refuse to worship the newborn, and say cheerful good riddance to the departing. For contemporary medieval and agrarian thinkers, the possibilities are marvelous. But this is more than a simple resurgence of agrarianism; it is industrial-strength agrarianism.

Lord Falkland once commented that when it was not necessary to change, it was necessary not to change. This aphorism is particularly appropriate on this question. Given where we are, any attempt to recreate a medieval society as it was would be the most unmedieval thing we could do. To make peace with plastics is not a compromise with modernity because modernity is never at peace with anything, including its own children. Modernity was born with revolutionary conflict and cannot sustain itself except through perpetual chaos and revolution against itself. The only cultural vision which can make peace with the blessings of modernity is . . . medievalism. The medievalist has the capacity, *and the desire,* to harmonize. He believes the planets sing in harmony; why cannot technology also sing? If technology is directed by men who know themselves to be created in the image of God—men who know themselves to be *men*—the problems begin to resolve themselves. As it stands now, technology is in the hands of men who believe themselves to be the products of a blind technology, made by that impersonal technocrat Darwinism. We are only machines, and we build machines, and why is everything around us so machine-like? The pride of modernity likes to ask the really deep questions.

Look at the arrogance of technopoly—the skyscraper, the outside covered with reptilian mirror-like scales. Look at the impressive design of the thing—a box set on its end. Now look at a medieval cathedral and explain to us all why you still believe in progress. The flying buttress was a technological marvel, but it was built by *men* who knew themselves to be such. Our skyscrapers were designed by empty men trying to forget their hollow chests. But it is not easy to forget the *imago Dei.*

So the problems with technology are not *resident* within the technology itself. To place any evil there is nothing but modernist superstition. Only a modernist could think that a machine was inherently good or evil. The earth is the Lord's and the fullness thereof. The problems are problems of idolatry, problems which are perpetually resident in the heart of man. The technology just sits there; the idolatry brings on the hype—e.g., all the falsehoods we are told about what the latest software will do for us. A very recent example of this is the exuberant tub-thumping for computers in education. We are told, *ad nauseam,* that a computer has to go into every classroom to prepare us for the twenty-first century. We have not yet realized that the computers may simply be moving our ignorance around the planet at incredible rates of speed. As one wag put it, "We used to think that a million monkeys typing away at a million keyboards could produce the works of Shakespeare. Now, thanks to the Internet, we know this is not the case." A fool in the back of a cart bumping along the road five hundred years ago is, today, a fool in the backseat of a Lexus. Certain things are not changed by the computerized dashboard.

Another problem coming from the heart of man is our desire to blindly bestow robes of authority, which, in our modern world, we have done to the scientists. The mystique of Science has bestowed on a certain class within our society the stature of priests. Only a madman would try to market headache medicine today under the name *John's Headache Pills.* This would be insufficiently techno-marvelous. No, the name must sound like it came out of a laboratory yesterday . . . *Zantistat 100,* or something like that.

None of this is to argue that technology is neutral. While neither good nor evil reside in technology, the ethical bias of technology certainly lends itself to certain temptations and errors. This bias is comparable to the bias of wealth. Scripture teaches that wealth is a blessing from God, and that we should seek to harmonize that blessing (when it is received) with full devotion to the God who richly gives us all things to enjoy. If we are to be scriptural, we cannot say that wealth is *malum in se,* wicked in itself. At the same time, the Bible is filled with stern warnings about the tendency which wealth has to make a man forget God. "And thou say in thine heart, 'My power and the might of mine hand hath gotten me this wealth.' But thou shalt remember the Lord thy God" (Deut. 8:17–18). We would all be surprised to find a scriptural warning to the rich, enjoining them to watch and guard themselves against their constant temptations to excessive humility. Wealth does not have the bias which normally creates that kind of temptation. Certain temptations go with wealth, even though wealth is not inherently sinful.

In some respects the temptations of technology are identical to the temptations which have always come with wealth—self-sufficiency, pride, insolence. Those who react to the pride of the wealthy with vows of poverty are not touching the problem, but rather reacting to it. In the same way, those who revolt against the stainless steel gleam of modernity with a reactionary wearing of grunge clothing are simply part of the larger context of modernity.

A true contrast would come from a medieval view of things. The medieval approach to technology would begin with profound gratitude for those things which are genuine blessings. A walk through a third-world meat market makes one grateful for refrigeration and shrink-wrapped food. Our children are much more likely to live longer than we will, and if they do so while loving the Lord, the great length of days will be a great blessing to them. This longevity and many associated blessings will be connected to, among many other things, laser surgeries and antibiotic soaps. The best antidote to the spirit of modernity is gratitude.

Secondly, a medievalist would refuse to worship at the shrines we have created which employ our priestly caste of scientists. When they produce something good and useful, we must be grateful for it. But we do not see them in the place of God, and neither do we think they can solve any problem if enough research dollars are poured into the effort. This is a long-standing problem, but part of the reason why we may be better prepared to do this presently is that our scientists have taken to saying things which are patently false—false even by their own standards. We used to believe them when they confidently spoke of this and that. Were they not speaking in the name of Modern Science? But their speculations about biological evolution have led to a great deal of hilarity among sensible observers, and a scientific approach to economics has led to all the wisdom we have come to expect from big government. This deterioration of scientific respectability has been overseen by genuine scientists who have overreached the legitimate boundaries of their various disciplines and have been furthered by their camp followers in the social studies who wanted to have official-looking white lab coats of their own. When the fuzzy disciplines started claiming the authority that is due to scientific precision, the results were not good for scientific credibility. The ranks of the scientific elite have been expanded far too rapidly to keep effective control of the masses, and many people are now aware of how funny science can be.

The third element necessary will be the employment of the fruits of technology in the cultural setting of middle earth. This is the hard work which will take many genera-tions. After a man has learned to think differently and has repudiated the lies of modernity, he still, for example, must endeavor to plow his land. How is that to be done? Is a mule necessary to medievalism? If machinery is used, is that a compromise? For those who have thought through the issue carefully, the answer is that technologically-advanced medi-evalism is no compromise. A man may accept some of the fruits of modernity in order to spur himself on in the work of building a medieval culture. But he must be careful to teach his sons.

CHAPTER 16

POETIC KNOWLEDGE

LEARNING TO BE POETICALLY ACTIVE

To this end they procured a royal patent for erecting an Academy of Projectors in Lagado. Every room hath in it one or more projectors. The first man I saw had been eight years extracting sunbeams out of cucumbers.

—Jonathan Swift

Learning to know poetically is at the heart of any true defiance of modernity and any genuine recovery of the medieval mind. Pascal called this kind of knowledge *esprit d'finesse*, the ability intuitively to grasp the meaning of the whole. Learning to name what we see with poetic authority, and to hear clearly what others have so named, is to learn the proper use of words. And to complete this somewhat cryptic introduction, because we men cannot be God, we must learn to be good poets.

Because we are creatures, we must necessarily see and express the world poetically. All our knowledge is in some fashion metaphorical. Only God knows things *immediately*. For us, wound tight in our finitude, knowledge of the world must be mediated, that is, apportioned to us the same way a toddler gets his mashed peas. Now in using this language of immediacy in God's knowledge, we are borrowing nothing from Descartes or any form of egocentric philosophy. This is simply a point in classical theology; God does not "find out" about things. As the great theologian Turretin expressed it, He sees "the various turns and changes of things by an immutable cognition."[1]

We are a different case. This means that all our communications are in some sense metaphorical or poetic. But, complicating it further, because we are sinners, much of what we express is *bad* poetry. In other words, while the modernist may deny he is necessarily a poet, this does not keep him from being one. What it does prevent is the possibility of his becoming any good at his craft. The medieval mind says that a man is jovial; the modernist says he is hardwired happy. Both can be taken as metaphorical expressions, but the former does the work with far more grace. The postmodernist, by embracing relativism, is pretending to reject modernism. But he continues to hold to the modernist view that poetry is essentially . . . meaningless. But God has told men to come to the absolute truth through metaphor, and so we must learn to do it.

The modernist way of knowing can be called various high-sounding things, one of them being Cartesian rationalism. But the world is an enchanted place, and so when a scientist describes it for us as a great concourse of atoms banging blindly down the corridors of time, we should not commend his stark scientific realism. We should rather condemn the clunky poetry. Lucretius at least had the decency to make it scan. Our choice is not between science and poetry, but rather between good poetry and bad poetry.

This problem is by no means limited to avowed materialists. For example, modern evangelicals (having swallowed the modernist *zeitgeist* whole and entire) like to compare holy

1. Turretin, *Institutes*, vol. 1, 207.

things to soft drinks, designer clothes, or whatever else, as long as it is some part of our modern consumerist culture. The problem with this is not the fact of the comparison to a created thing. The problem is that it is ham-handedly bad poetry and therefore disrespectful and impudent poetry. The Bible compares God to very mundane things, but does so with poetic wonder. God "shall come down like rain upon the mown grass: as showers that water the earth" (Ps. 72:6).

If someone were to claim that the forgiveness of Christ clears the head like a really good nasal spray, the problem is one of a tin ear, and *not* the introduction of noses into the discussion of spiritual things. "Then the channels of waters were seen, and the foundations of the world were discovered at thy rebuke, O Lord, at the blast of the breath of thy nostrils" (Ps. 18:15). The Bible tells us that Christ is the lion of the tribe of Judah, but it also tells us not to change the glory of the incorruptible God into an image of a four-footed beast—say, like a lion (Rom. 1:22–23). The eye of the Lord follows all those who fear Him, and underneath are the everlasting arms. But how the deuce can an incorporeal Spirit have eyes and arms? Such questions will always be asked . . . by bad poets.

So our task is that of recovering an epistemology of poetry, and, having done so, we may come to see how important the love of good poetry is. The true poet is one who has learned to think and speak of God humbly and the creation obliquely, knowing what he does.

Man is not God and cannot be. This much is self-evident, and few would dispute the point openly. But sinful men still desire what they cannot say they desire and constantly try to assume the divine prerogatives, all the while not admitting their ambition to be such. But such fools are aspiring to a great height. "Great is our Lord, and of great power:

his understanding is *infinite*" (Ps. 147:5). At the heart of the modernist idolatry is the assumption that autonomous man can have an understanding which successfully reaches toward this—to know exhaustively or truly, or both.

All modern men have an implicit epistemology, and that epistemology is an arrogant scientific rationalism. In other words, they assume that things are only to be "known" in accord with the dictates of "science." Through science, mankind collectively wants to attain to this divine kind of knowledge in two ways. One, they aspire to omniscience. This cannot, of course, be done, but it *can* be pretended. When Man as Priest/Scientist speaks—whether about the health dangers of margarine or the internal temperature of supernovas does not matter—he likes to speak *ex cathedra*. This is accepted by a well-conditioned public with great docility, but a thinking man will read each new breathless scientific announcement with a bemused detachment. "I wonder how much there remains to this subject which they do *not* know?"

Or modern man can seek a God-like knowledge in his demand for what the philosophers call epistemic certainty in a particular area. They may not know everything, but what they do know, they want to know *perfectly*. Of course neither kind of divine knowledge is possible for finite and sinful men. We do not share God's knowledge in extent, and we do not know in the same way He does. As creatures, our knowledge is *finite*, and it is *mediated*.

The desire to know all things perfectly is the desire to be God. But men cannot know in this way. "For my thoughts are not your thoughts, neither are your ways my ways, saith the Lord. For as the heavens are higher than the earth, so are my ways higher than your ways, and my thoughts than your thoughts" (Is. 55:8–9). The Scriptures tell us in many places that God's thoughts are beyond our reach, and beyond our comprehension. "O the depth of the riches both of the wisdom and knowledge of God! how unsearchable are his judgments, and his ways past finding out!" (Rom. 11:33; cf. 1 Cor. 2:10–11).

But when in our idolatry of ourselves we grasp after this kind of knowledge, the result is not the attainment of Deity, but rather the distortion of the creature. In other words, when we imitate what we *think* is perfection, the result is just a bent caricature. One such distorted imitation is the pristine, stainless steel box that we call modernity. But this is not our assigned habitat; this in not how we were told to live. A fruit-bearing tree runs just as well as a diesel genera-tor, just not on the same principles. Christ told His disciples to bear much fruit, not to generate lots of amperage. The soul of modernity is a Cartesian rationalism, and since the rise of that paradigm as an all-encompassing way of think-ing about everything, we have managed to suck the soul out of all our images. This has not annihilated the images—we cannot function apart from them—but it has left them bent and twisted on the ground. We are still poetic, but our po-etry has been languishing for three hundred years.

Modernity is part of the air we breathe, it shapes the way we think. So it is not enough to reject evil factories, urban blight, and our massive consumption-driven culture. We are moderns in our virtues as well as our vices. We are mod-erns in what makes us proud and not just in what makes us ashamed. This means that an essential part of the way back is repenting of our glory. The modernist, in the grip of sci-entism, emphasizes precision through engineering, straight-forward quantification, authoritative abstraction, and direct correlation to the material, physical realm in everything he does. He wants to treat the entire world as though it were a box of machined parts, or Tinker Toys—little pieces of wood that stick together with other pieces of wood. This works well in building suspension bridges, but it is one of the worst epistemologies that can be conceived.

By contrast, poetic knowledge, which is essential to a recovery of the medieval mind, values precision through imprecision, extensive *sic et non* qualification, authoritative concrete images, and oblique correlations of wisdom to the creation. And this because we can never know if we have handled a poem as well as a multiplication table, which brings us to consider the characteristics of what may be called the poetic mind.

First, the poetic mind cultivates knowledge through an exaltation of Christ. Without Christ there is no *arche,* no final point of integration. We are told in Colossians that Christ is the One in whom all things hold together. The modern approach to knowledge is like gathering and dropping ten thousand BB's on a tile floor. If someone objects to the resultant chaos, the proposed modern solution is to apply for a federal grant to acquire thousands more BB's, throw *them* down and see if it helps. But in Christ nothing is isolated, nothing is separated, nothing is detached. In Christ, *nothing* is random. This means that any part of the universe may help me speak of another part.

Beginning here with the love of Christ reminds us of a point made elsewhere in this book, which is best summarized with the phrase *beauty of holiness.* We do not worship Christ as a mere abstracted Point of Integration, but rather we love Him as our Creator and Savior. This permeates everything which follows and is well characterized as the love of all things lovely. When Christ is loved, loveliness is diffused throughout all creation and all interaction with it.

Secondly, the poetic mind cultivates knowledge "by addition." This involves a rejection of Hellenistic thinking which seeks to know through "subtraction." The modern world is Hellenistic at this point, trying to find the essence of a thing by taking away all its external attributes. Then, when the essential thing is finally found, naked and shivering, we assume we have gotten down to the defined "reality." But the poetic mind tries to understand by means of addition. A thing is described from first this aspect, and then from that one. This characteristic is named, and then that one. Layer upon layer of description is added. A bird is understood when it is named on the wing and not when it is stuffed and mounted in a glass case at the Smithsonian, or, worse still, when its essential birdness is isolated in a wildlife textbook or dictionary.

Related to this, we must understand that reality faces *out*. What we see is what God gave us. Neither the mind of the rationalist, nor the mystic gut of the Romantic, can disassemble the world to find out what it is really like "inside" what is revealed. We are not competent to take anything apart to find out what is inside. The analytic paradigm wants to find meaning in the pieces, and the Romantic simply tries to take the thing apart differently. The poetic mind seeks to find the meaning of a thing in its attributes, which are known "on the outside." Now of course the poetic mind can speak of knowing something on the "inside" but it does not confuse this helpful metaphor with some philosophical reality.

Third, the poetic mind cultivates knowledge through authoritative naming. Although we have no authority where God has not granted it, we do have a great deal where He has. The first task assigned to Adam was to name the animals, and there is more in this than one might suppose. A great part of our work in the world is that of covenantal naming. The detached scientist assumes that his duty is to watch the world grind away, and then, as a neutral observer, to record what he has seen. He wants to see what it is and then name it. It never occurs to him that he has authority beyond this—that is, to name something and through that naming, to shape it.

For example, the modernist historian wants to make his determination based upon the dictates of science—quantitative, detailed, meticulous analysis. The modernist historian wants to count and quantify everything and does not believe he may name until he has discovered the real name "inside" the subject he studies. But a poet can read through an account of the battle of First Manassas, and say that Stonewall Jackson was the epitome of Southern manhood. And he was.

All reality is covenantal, which means that it must be handled through its "covenant representatives." This is what a metaphor *is*. And so the man with a poetic mind does not hesitate to name. He exercises dominion through naming. He is a covenant lord, and he is assigning covenantal authority as he names. It is the same with art, which provides us with another example. A man who paints a picture of a bowl of apples is not maintaining that we have a shortage of apples. He is saying that we have a shortage of *understanding* apples, and this is why he has given them another name. We have not yet understood apples the way that we ought.

But we must be obedient in our naming, seeking to be stewards of God in the world. We cannot name blindly, or name things just to conceal our helplessness—e.g., with names like *gravity* or *zero* or *infinity*. The result of such flailing will be that we ignorantly maintain that things fall down because gravity pulls them, zero is a *number* between one and negative one, and infinity is just as big as two infinities. This is not to say that such names and the "things" they represent have no place in our thinking. The point is simply that careful thought must accompany naming. We must always remember that God has named everything already.

Fourth, the poetic mind cultivates knowledge by means of growth and gradual accumulation. We are not born desiring truth, but rather milk. Truth is not found primarily through the reflections of trained philosophers and scientists. It is found primarily through faithful mothers diligently spanking bottoms. We are designed and created by God to grow up into truth. The idea that we could ever dispassionately approach the search for truth with a detached Cartesian spirit is an idea which dies hard. We must learn our theology and worldview from the high chair, and, more than this, we must learn that this is how we are supposed to learn them.

In the providence of God, He did not start us out with detached propositions about Him; He began us with a mother's breast. We are creatures federally connected; true thinking begins in the cradle and before. John leapt with joy in his mother's womb, and from the lips of nursing infants God has ordained praise—and this, not as a cute Kodak moment, but rather to silence the foe and the avenger.

A great need exists for Christians to begin to think through the ramifications of their faith in both a systematic and practical way. We must put off childish things and think like men. Christianity is a serious and demanding religion, and this includes the intellectual ramifications of that faith. However, part of mature thinking about the faith is the understanding that all mature thought grows out of immature thought, and that this process is gradual and continual. Wesley spoke well of the firstborn seraph trying to make sense of it all, but we are not like that privileged celestial being. Conceived in sin, speaking lies from the womb, trusting in God from the breast, our apportioned lot is very different.

When we have come of age, we should look back on the process and see that where we came from does not define who God is. God reveals Himself to the mature mind as ultimate and transcendent. Our experience does not contain Him or define Him. But His sovereign majesty does contain our experience. In Him we live and move and have our being. The God revealed in Scripture brought us up from nothing into the dim consciousness of life in the womb, then into the bright light and fluctuating temperatures outside and then to the comforting milk and then to the crawling around which soon bumps into authority, and then years later . . . epistemology proper.

Fifth, the poetic mind cultivates precise knowledge by means of imprecision. This is not an attempt to be cute, or to blur the picture—but rather to make it clear. The world has been constituted in such a way that precise statements about it are frequently . . . incomplete and imprecise. Words are not integers, with precise mathematical equivalents. When a man learns precision of language and clarity of thought, he does not accomplish it by imitating algebra. *The rain touched the petal* cannot be adequately reduced to *R implies P(t)*. Some of the content can be placed into symbolic notation, but nowhere near all of it. The modernist wants high algebraic certainty, but this always gives him a low return.

My girlfriend is quite pretty is a straightforward statement, simple to understand, and yet it tells us far less than *My love is like a red, red rose.* Or, to take another example, *God is immutable* is entirely accurate and precise, and yet it tells us less than the statement *God is like a mountain, never changing.* The second statement is less precise in terms of scientific theology, but at the same time it accurately conveys much more of the truth—to the one who understands poetry. But how can something which is "less true" communicate "more truth?"

This is how God, in the wisdom of God, presents the world to us. Our knowledge of God must be analogical, which is another way of saying that it must be poetical. Our knowledge of the creation functions in the same way, because this is how we were created to think.

But when precision as understood by scientists and engineers becomes the template for understanding everything, problems immediately follow. With mathematical processes, the level of certainty is high. However, because of the narrowness and inflexibility of the instruments, the scope of certainty is truncated, and our knowledge of the *fullness* of creation begins to hemorrhage.

We have taken this valuable but truncated way of reading a very narrow aspect of general revelation and turned it into a way of reading everything. For example, because an engineering solution in the natural world requires us to solve the math problem out to the tenth decimal place, we then either assume with the liberal that the Bible has errors in it or we rise to the challenge as modernist conservatives and do detailed word studies out to the tenth decimal place in order to "engineer" the solution to the infidel challenge. Sadly, this is done both by hack exegetes in the pulpit and renowned scholars in the original tongues. The problem here is that both infidel and believers, whether educated and uneducated, are modernists to the bone.

But words do not have decimal places. Neither do flowers and volcanoes. The eye can see but cannot do logarithms. A toddler can catch a ball but cannot do the math necessary to enable him to do so. Symbols or numbers in a mathematical formula have a denotation but no connotation to speak of. The number 28 does not have the same aroma as, say, the word *tepid*, which is what ice cubes become when they decide to become a dull and uninteresting glass of water. This means that the information about the word conveyed through such symbols is *skeletal at best*. The problem we face is that we have come to assume that our abstractions of reality's skeleton are, in fact, reality itself. And this is why our precisionist minds are so confused. All around us this *extra* stuff is flying by.

Sixth, the poetic mind cultivates knowledge by means of concrete images. This is one of the central characteristics of poetry. With this in mind, Sir Philip Sidney contrasted the two ways of learning.

> Anger, the *Stoicks* says, was a short madness: let but *Sophocles* bring you *Ajax* on a stage, killing and whipping Sheepe and Oxen, thinking them the Army of *Greeks,* with theyr Chiefetaines *Agamemnon* and *Menelaus,* and tell mee if you have not a more familiar insight into anger then finding in the Schoolmen his *Genus* and Difference.[2]

For example, a preacher may say that sins should not be indulged, including secret sins. Or he may refer, more effectively, to tolerated sins, like so many mice in the walls of your mind. The latter image is striking and concrete. It is also less "accurate" than the earlier abstract statement, but it communicates more truth. Those who strive for the "safe" and abstract succeed only in producing bland poetry. Those who risk something in selecting a concrete image may fail, but at least they clearly failed at *poetry*.

This also means the poetic mind cultivates love for the right word. Someone may get the idea that because concrete images are good, all he has to do is deck his language out in some lurid fashion. He has avoided blandness in his expression but this does not keep it from being bad. Adam was created speaking, and our responsibility is to further our sanctification by learning to speak well.

2. Sir Philip Sydney, *Defence of Poesy, Astrophil and Stella, and Other Writings* (London: Everyman, 1997), 95.

Seventh, surprisingly, the poetic mind protects knowledge by means of an analytic fence. The poetic mind rejects the analytic *paradigm;* the poetic mind does not reject the gift of analysis. The ability to make careful distinctions does not exist as a result of the fall. God has given us our abilities of abstraction for a good and honorable purpose. The point being made in this chapter is simply that the analytic mind was not created to serve as an epistemology.

But one of the valuable functions of analytic, precisionist language is that of protecting poetic expression. For example, this is why creeds must be precise and will necessarily and naturally drift toward a language which some might think is "theological engineering." Athanasius and Arius differ over the precise definition of *homoousia* and *homoiousia,* and in that distinguishing iota the future of Western civilization was bound up. That momentous struggle was about whether or not Jesus of Nazareth was God, and the difference of opinion had to be revealed in such a fashion. The two men would not have differed at all over an unprotected poetic statement such as, "Jesus Christ has ascended the mount of all strength," but the lack of disagreement would not have meant concord.

This is why, for example, when the liberal Presbyterian Church adopted their new and improved creed in the sixties, the move away from precision of language was entirely a bad thing. Their creedal language was more "scriptural" and "poetic," which in such a confessional context was horrible. Scriptural language in certain contexts is rebellion against God.

Liars are experts in chopping logic and missing the truth *slightly*—"Did God say not to eat from *any* tree?" In order to pin a liar down, words must be defined in the most careful manner available. In this context, the only man who needs to be more precise than a liar is the man who would catch the liar. This is why people who hate the Bible say they want the language of the Bible, not the language of creeds, and why men who faithfully apply a faithful creed (containing words and language found nowhere in Scripture), are doing exactly what the Bible requires of them. "Thou has tried them which say" (Rev. 2:2). The nature of the testing can and should include very carefully crafted verbal formulae designed to trip up the dishonest. "And every spirit that confesseth not that Jesus Christ is come in the flesh is not of God" (1 Jn. 4:3).

The poetic mind takes the world the way it was given. Poetic knowledge presents a great opportunity for those who love the truth, carefully set apart. We are told that an honest answer is like a kiss on the lips. Reading the world around us, we realize that the ambiguities resident there are an opportunity for much dishonesty—or, for the pure in mind, for honesty. Ignoring the subtlety of the creation, a dishonest man may ignore what he sees by means of close and careful scrutiny (Jn. 5:39). So creeds should be a door to keep all such dishonest men out. And then the table may be set for honest men within.

Cough syrup is not wine, not even the red kind. In a fallen world, such measures are necessary and good. But even in a fallen world, such measures are still a response to sin and not a *positive* good. An iron fence needs to be built around the garden. But if we are concerned for *all* truth, we must never confuse iron posts with vegetables. This fence functions primarily as a screen to keep certain vandals and marauders *out*. For example, we must say that God is immutable. This communicates a lot of valuable information, very little of it about God directly. This tells us more about what God is *not* than about what He is. I know that the statement *God is immutable* is one hundred percent truth, but this puts us in possession of a one-hundred-percent truth which is not very big. But this small truth excludes a multitude of lies, *and this is the value of it*. I have no direct understanding of immutability, but I have much experience with mutability. I know what mutability is like, and God is not like that. The same is true of finitude. I know what it is, and yet I have no earthly idea what infinitude is. But God is infinite, that is, He is not like the bounded things I know and understand.

We adopt these iron post words to build our fence so that heretics will not pillage the garden. Precisionist, creedal language serves this valuable function.

> O Timothy, *keep* that which is committed to thy trust, avoiding profane and vain babblings and oppositions of science falsely so called: Which some professing have erred concerning the faith. Grace be with thee. Amen. (1 Tim. 6:20–21)

So by this we protect the language of orthodox and poetic devotion. What we say inside the fence is frequently inconsistent with the fence itself. This is fine, and necessary, but it must be done *inside* the fence of creedal orthodoxy. If anyone within begins using language the same way heretics outside the fence do, then they must be expelled. While poetic language cannot protect itself, precisionist language by itself leaves nothing worth protecting. So we keep and tend our creeds, so that we may compose and sing our hymns—always remembering that in heaven the hymns will be the thing.

Eighth, the poetic mind cultivates knowledge by means of humility. God is the only Law-giver. This means we must be extraordinarily careful whenever we indignantly prescribe anything. A good example of our modernist hubris here is our attitude toward the rules of grammar and associated lexical subjects. The poetic mind does not approach language with pursed, censorious lips. Our repeated attempts to place a pristine set of rules on top of how people actually use language is a very clear example of our desire to play Moses on some lexical Sinai. For example, we give ourselves to schoolmarmish severities, and tell people not to end sentences with a preposition. That, as Churchill said, is the sort of nonsense up with which we shall not put. That particular rule was applied out of the blue by those who thought English should want to be more like Latin. In Latin a sentence cannot end in a preposition. But down here in the fleshpots of Egypt we find the bawdiness of English. Get English to conform to Latin grammar? But this is like deciding that a human skeleton is superior to a dog's skeleton, and consequently trying to teach your dog to walk like a man.

Of course we may prescribe in a very humble and limited way. If we tell someone not to use the salad fork to pick his teeth, we are only watching out for his social interests. We want him to be invited back again. We might tell someone not to say *Me and her came down for the interview* if the interview in question is for a position teaching English. We are only trying to help him get the job.

But only God truly knows English. Are the rules of grammar descriptive or prescriptive? This is a false dilemma; they are inadequately both. Only God can describe English, and He hasn't, and only God has the authority to prescribe absolutely, and He didn't. We want to assert that the learning of grammar is the key to mastery, when actually mastery is the key to grammar.

To overstate the case a little, a man does not have mastery of a word unless he is *unable* to tell you how he knows what it means. Every word we use in knowledge has countless little dents in it. A word will age over time, not only in an individual's use of it, but also in a culture's use of it. Words will morph into other words. The meaning of a word will never be found shivering alone in its birthday suit. We cannot ever act as though the essential meanings of words were hermit crabs, crawling from one home to another. The majority of what you have learned, with profit, you cannot recall, which is probably just as well.

Ninth, the poetic mind cultivates knowledge through careful balance and harmony. We are to live and act in the world; we are not to react. It was Nietzsche who pointed out that men alternate between the rational Apollonian approach and the wild and crazy Dionysian approach. Men adopt one stance because they are tired of the previous one. But after a short stay *there,* nothing seems to work out, and it is time to careen back to the former set of problems. Stability in this scenario is not an option. Men who do not know God must always lurch and wobble.

For example, the Romantics reacted to neo-Classicism of the late seventeenth and eighteenth centuries. The neo-Classical approach was precisionist, meticulous, rationalistic and fussy, and so the Romantics in reaction were mystical, sentimental, carefree, and emotional. What we are pleased to call "the sixties" was the same kind of thing. The hippies were just another wave of Dionysians. But unlike previous Dionysians, we *were* distinguished by one thing. Because our generation had been so badly educated in government schools, we thought this process, old as dirt, actually represented Something New and Fresh in the World. It was the Age of Aquarius and all of that.

The poetic mind seeks to understand the world as God gave it, not react to the world as understood by the previous generation of boneheads. Reaction is always good for a quick following, but it is no good at all in building a civilization. So the poetic mind is not Romanticism—Romanticism was a reaction to the earlier Apollonian establishment. The poetic mind understands that reality presents three aspects to us—the true, the good, and the lovely—and receives it as such.

But the Romantic thinks of the aesthetic experience as the one door into the house of reality. So he comes in the door marked lovely, believing that the rooms true and good will be found upstairs and down the hall. The rationalist does the same thing, only he thinks the door is labeled differently—he thinks it is the door of reason and truth. The moralist of course does the same, thinking the entryway is the good. But the poetic mind does not understand any of these three aspects of reality as the "key" to the rest.

Tenth, the poetic mind cultivates knowledge through submission to canonical authority. Our experience of poetry, and the poetic nature of all reality, is not individualistic. We are attached to one another, and we are connected to those who have lived before us. Those who will be descended from us will be in the same position.

Because we are connected with one another, we should seek to preserve our understanding of those connections. This means communicating with one another, and over time, this means reading one another's books. However, a brief walk through Barnes & Noble should make you wonder why every other person you know isn't an author. We must read, but there is too much to read. Consequently, if we want our reading to be cultural communication, and not just entertainment, we should take care that our reading is canonical.

The poetic mind cultivates the cultural cadences of the mind. In the West, this means reading and rereading the Authorized Version of the Bible. It means Shakespeare and Milton and Homer and Vergil and other worthies in the Western canon. Without a canonical understanding *belles-lettres*, a man's poetic expressions cannot be paid out in the coin of the realm.

One of the great developments in the Middle Ages was the clash between the older tradition in philosophy called realism and the distinctively Christian development of a tradition called nominalism. Because this development occurred at a time when the authority of Christ was still acknowledged, the resultant nominalism was a great advance in understanding the world God gave us to live in.

But with the arrival of modernity came secularism, and the debate between realism and nominalism continued . . . in an unreal and desacralized world. Abstractions like this never make sense considered apart from Christ. God reveals Himself in creation, culminating in the Incarnation. We must start all our thinking with the revelation of Christ as the ultimate revelation. Christless realism tries to find a transcendent *arche* based upon the obvious need for one coupled with the speculations of the philosophers. Christless nominalism has all the bricks, but no mortar. But because Jesus is Lord, all things hold together, including lost men, under the authority of His Word. But that which binds all things together is the Word, not the Equation. The world is a revelatory gift, not a code to be deciphered.

When Paul describes membership in the Church, he does not speak of membership in our modern sense. He does not show us one member of the Kiwanas compared to another one, but rather the ankle of man's body compared to his lips. When we learn to think about the world this way, no longer will a pastor want to be like the CEO of General Motors, or a mother like a mother board of a computer, or a secretary like a ball-bearing in a smoothly running office. "Herein is my Father glorified, that ye bear much fruit; so shall ye be my disciples" (Jn. 15:8). Poetic learning considers and understands the whole as a series of growing, living interrelationships.

So modern man must stop for a moment and consider the teaching of the Savior. Having done so, he should ask himself this question: How is it possible to live like a machine and bear fruit like a tree? If the question does not shake his timbers, what goeth on in the world, he wots not.

CHAPTER 17

A SECOND CHRISTENDOM

FROM THE RIVER TO THE ENDS OF THE EARTH

[S]uch love shall arise
And such a peace among the people and a perfect trust
That Jews shall judge in their wit—and be joyful at heart
—That Moses or Messiah has come to middle earth,
And have marvel in their minds that men are so true.

—William Langland, *Piers Plowman*

Before Jesus ascended into heaven, He assigned an apparently overwhelming task to His disciples. "And Jesus came and spake unto them, saying, All power is given unto me in heaven and in earth. Go ye therefore, and teach all nations, baptizing them in the name of the Father, and of the Son, and of the Holy Ghost: teaching them to observe all things whatsoever I have commanded you: and, lo, I am with you alway, *even* unto the end of the world. Amen" (Mt. 28:18–20). Like many familiar words, these often just float by us. We think we understand them simply because we are accustomed to them.

But an understanding of this passage must always be at the center of any thought of a distinctively Christian culture—not because our Lord's words are primarily concerned with politics, but because they are *not*. Following the Lord's

authority, one of the distinctives of Christian cultural understanding is that it also is minimally concerned with politics.
The restoration of the nations is not, in any important sense,
a political process. Rather, the process is one of baptism and
catechism. The means given for the conversion of the hea-
then were the waters of baptism and the words of instruction.
When the lessons have been learned, there will of course be
some political consequences. But they will be minimal for
the simple reason that the state itself, in a nation that has
come to repentance, will also be minimal. For the Christian,
the political realm is a creature to be redeemed, sinful like
the rest of us and with a long way to go before it retires to
more biblical proportions.

A return to a medieval manner of thinking therefore
means recovering what, for a modernist, is almost an anar-
chic mentality. We have lived in the cocoon of modern statism for so long that we believe that nothing—anarchy—is
outside of it. As we have seen, God has established those
authorities which exist in their separate realms and has
placed set bounds for them. But because there is no ultimacy
in middle earth, modernist idolaters react. In just the way
that early Christians were accused of atheism because they
did not worship the gods, so medieval Protestants will be
accused of anarchy because we will not pledge allegiance to
the flags. Let it be so.

The state is certainly no redeemer and political theory no
savior. The medieval mind would be highly suspicious of the
abstractionist social engineer, adept in the ways of political
theory. One of the problems with pure political theory is that
humble people, long traditions, and ancient customs tend to
get in the way of the Grand Idea, and the impatient theorist
wants to cut all such *impedimenta* to fit the theory. Good
sense would rather modify or abandon the theory to fit the

way the living God made and governs the world. As Christians, when we consider our cultural condition, we are to take the flow of God's providence over history into account and resist the ever-present temptations of political solutions. The one nation we were never told to disciple is Utopia, and there is no political remedy for the disease we have.

Our problems are spiritual, and the solutions are the Word and sacraments. The charge was not "go ye, and elect right-of-center congresspersons." Now certainly the gospel has an effect on all of culture, as it should. But results are not causes; apples are not roots.

In our history, as the gospel spread throughout the Gentile world, *of course* it began to have a cultural and civic impact. How could it not? The eventual cultural effect of this was Christendom—a motley collection of nations which together, with varying degrees of success, acknowledged the Lordship of Jesus Christ over them. Beginning with the time of Constantine, warts and blemishes were plentiful, but there were glorious times in Christendom as well. But the spiritual history of these once-converted nations is now, it seems, just history. The modern secularist gloats—"The days of your Christendom are over and done. Thanks to reason and science, we have put all that safely behind us."

It is safe to say that with the birth of materialistic secularism, the publication of Darwin's *Origin of Species,* the rise of industrial statism, the arrogance of militant unbelief, and the cultural retreat of virtually all believing Christians—in short the triumph of modernity—this vaunt of the secularist appears to be warranted. The issue appears to be settled. When the Confederate States of America surrendered at Appomattox, the last nation of the older order fell. So, because historians like to have set dates on which to hang their hats, we may say the first Christendom died there, in

1865. The American South was the last nation of the first Christendom.

But the *idea* of Christendom has not passed away. God's promise remains. He has promised that all the nations will come to His Son, and He has carefully instructed us to teach them this. When the kings turn to us inquiringly, we are to tell them to kiss the Son, lest He be angry with them (Ps. 2:12). Christians should therefore not be despondent when we do not see this happening on our schedule, or our timetable. The Psalm says that kings should be worried about the anger of the Lord, not that the Lord's followers should be worried about the footdragging of kings.

Our father in the faith, the ancestor of this glorious ingathering of nations, gives us a wonderful basis for faith whenever we see the cause of the godly "die."

> For the promise, that he should be *the heir of the world*, was not to Abraham, or to his seed, through the law, but through the righteousness of faith. . . . even God, *who quickeneth the dead*, and calleth those things which be not *as though they were:* who against hope believed in hope, that he might become the father of many nations, according to that which was spoken, "So shall thy seed be." (Rom. 4:13–18)

As the gospel makes its way through a treacherous world, we have seen the righteous fall many times, and before the Lord comes again, we will see them fall again. But whenever the righteous fall, those who lament must be sons of Abraham. They must serve the God who calls those things that do not exist as though they did. Our God raises the dead. This truth is not an obscure and peripheral dogma; it is at the center of our faith—Christ rose from the dead. This also is at the center of our hope—the nations will come, and those that have fallen will come back again.

This means there will be a second Christendom, and if necessary, then a third. The Lord taught us to expect the process to be a gradual one—as leaven works through the loaf, as a mustard seed grows—but the Word teaches just as surely that the process is an inexorable one. "And in that day there shall be a root of Jesse, which shall stand for an ensign of the people; to it shall the Gentiles seek: and his rest shall be glorious" (Is. 11:10). And the psalmist promises us this: "All the ends of the world shall remember and turn unto the Lord: and all the kindreds of the nations shall worship before thee. For the kingdom is the Lord's: and he is the governor among the nations" (Ps. 22:27–28). John the Apostle tells us of the same things. "And the nations of them which are saved shall walk in the light of it: and the kings of the earth do bring their glory and honour into it" (Rev. 21:24).

Jesus did not teach us to pray, saying, "Thy kingdom come, Thy will be done in heaven if and when we get there." In His commission He told us to disciple *nations*. Empowered by the Spirit, this is done with the water of baptism and the rigorous teaching of the Word. In our prayers, Jesus told us to pray for the heavenly commonwealth to have an earthly manifestation. In short, we are to pray for Christendom.

These prayers will be answered, so this means that the South will rise again. But this is not said with any regional or national jingoistic fervor. So will New England rise again. So will Scotland. So will the Netherlands. And as the gospel comes to the uttermost regions for the first time, savage tribes will attend His word. The earth is the Lord's and He *will* have it. All these things will happen prior to the Second Advent. "The Lord said unto my Lord, 'Sit thou at my right hand, *until* I make thine enemies thy footstool'" (Ps. 110:1). After the Lord Jesus completed His perfect work of salvation, He ascended into heaven, and on clouds of glory

He approached the Ancient of Days. The Lord Christ, the Great High Priest, presented His perfect sacrifice to God the Father. It was received with great rejoicing, and the Son of God was granted His inheritance of universal and complete dominion over all the sons of men. Scripture presents this truth to us in the vision it gives of Christ, seated at the right hand of the Father. Every tribe, every nation, every people must now submit to Him. Every knee must bend before Him, and every tongue must confess that He alone is worthy of our worship and service.

In the wisdom of God it was ordained that this dominion of the Lord Jesus Christ would not be manifested instantaneously. As yeast works through a loaf of bread, the kingdom of God will slowly permeate all the nations of men, and peace will come to middle earth. As the rock cut without hands grows and becomes a mountain that fills the entire earth, so the kingdom of God will grow and subdue everything before it. As the water flows out from under the threshold of the temple, getting deeper and deeper as it goes, so the living water of the gospel of Christ flows from the New Temple until it fills the earth as the waters cover the sea, and *all* will know the Lord.

Now the Lord Christ took His seat at the right hand of the Father two millennia ago. He is seated there now, and Scripture tells us that He will remain there until all His enemies are beneath His feet. He is King of kings and Lord of lords; as temporal kings and lords progressively acknowledge this truth, His enemies collapse before Him. But how will they come to acknowledge such a thing? Will it be through political action or social involvement? No, the scepter in the hand of the Lord is the gospel of Christ in the mouths of His preachers. As they declare in faith who the Lord is and what He has done, the Lord sovereignly and majestically and efficaciously works in the hearts of unconverted men, and they are changed by His grace.

We have this confidence because our Lord and Savior did not come into the world to condemn the world. Nor did He come into the world to try to avoid condemning the world if He only could. His purpose in coming to our rebellious world was to save it. And His passion on the cross will not be seen to have accomplished its principal purpose until the world is saved. This is a promise of Scripture that our anemic modern church has long forgotten. We have abandoned the Great Commission through redefinition; this is one of our most grievous sins against the Lord. As His people, we of all people should know and acknowledge that Christ is Lord of all. Was it not promised to Abraham that all nations would be blessed through Him? This does not mean all the nations of men will be thrown into hell for rejecting Him—rather it means that His conquering cross, His efficacious redemption, will overcome their hatred of His holiness and their rejection of His kingdom.

Do we somehow think that He, rejected by men, went back into the heavens to sulk about it? Do we think that rebellious mankind has frustrated His declared intention and purpose? The Scriptures tell us nothing of this kind of defeatist dreaming. He went away, but He has not left us here alone and powerless. He has sent His Spirit to enable us to do what He commands from His throne. And what has He commanded? Did He want us to evangelize a few Pakistanis? A handful of Chinese? A tiny number of Russians? Though we might like to think in such limited terms, His command was for us to disciple the nations. He has commanded the Church, in His name and on His authority, to conquer the world through the fearless proclamation of the New Covenant that He has established with His people through His blood.

As we look at the world around us, it is easy to lose heart. But this does not excuse us, for it is our principal sin—we look at the world to determine what is possible instead of looking in faith to the risen Christ, seated with the Father. When the ten spies came back from spying out the land, they were not praised for their faintheartedness. We should not expect praise for the same species of faintheartedness.

Our common notion is that Christ came into the world to give saving the world a good effort. But Christ came into the world to drive the prince of this world *out*. He came and suffered in order to draw all men to Himself. Again, He came into the world, not to condemn the world, but to save it. We, with more exegetical nerve than responsibility, have turned this into the wistful dream of a forlorn Christ, rather than what the Bible declares it to be—the finished work of the conquering Christ. The Christ of modern evangelicalism is sitting at the right hand of the Father, but unfortunately He is on the edge of His seat, wringing His hands over the world's unwillingness to be saved by Him. Of course the world is unwilling! That is why He died—to overcome and conquer and subdue and destroy that unwillingness. Has He done it? The Bible says that He has. We like to think He has not, and our repentance is long overdue.

The day is coming, and now is, when God will make His people willing in the day of His power. Preachers of the gospel of Christ will declare, in power and faith, the message of grace to every nation, in every tongue. Do we have the eyes to see this? It depends entirely on where and how we look— and that depends upon the graciousness of the Father to us. This is a truth which can be seen only by faith, and this faith comes from hearing the Word of God. It does not come from pouring over newspapers for signs of the end, and not from gazing at the sky, feverishly trying to calculate the time of the end. Nor will it come from panicked reaction to the lies and stories of the most current false prophets and teachers.

This is a faith that comes from God; it can be seen only as God the Holy Spirit illuminates the teaching of Scripture. But once God has given us eyes to see this wonderful truth, it can be seen from any vantage point. This is because Christ has been lifted and exalted above every name, and He is therefore visible throughout the world—the world that will be saved. We know that this will happen because in the efficacious cross of Christ, the world has already been saved. And in turn this means we must pray for the resurgence of Christendom.

Many Christians veer into one of two errors in their view of future history. Either they plunge into a very exciting study of the pop eschatology and become consumed with the book of Revelation and newspaper reports about the European Union, trouble in the Middle East, and so forth, or they dismiss the whole thing with a wave of the hand and a joke. But much more is involved in this subject than the particular "chronology" we set for the events at the end of the world. Christians must come to understand that our doctrine of the power of the cross really is at the heart of our doctrine of the future history of the human race. Without the cross, there is no Christendom.

"And we have seen and do testify that the Father sent the Son to be the Saviour of the world" (1 Jn. 4:14). The Apostle John tells us that he, and others with him, have seen something and they testify to it. Now our duty as Christians is to stand with the apostles and join our witness to theirs. But how can we, if we do not see what they saw? And how can we testify to something we have not seen? They saw that the

Father sent the Son with a particular purpose in mind—this is the will of the Father to which Christ was submitting in the garden when He prepared to go to the cross. The Father sent the Son *as the Savior of the world.* The words are very plain, and words very much like them are found throughout all Scripture. This is the apostolic witness.

"And if any man hear my words, and believe not, I judge him not: for I came not to judge the world, but to save the world" (Jn. 12:47). Now Jesus seems to think that He did *not* come to judge the world. But most Christians think Jesus mistaken at this point—they think He will in fact condemn the world. We see the same thing in a very famous passage indeed. "For God so loved the world, that he gave his only begotten Son, that whosoever believeth in him should not perish, but have everlasting life. For God sent not his Son into the world to condemn the world; but that the world through him might be saved" (Jn. 3:16–17). The reason Christ came into the world was to save it . . . and most emphatically not to try to save it. The untutored Samaritans in John's gospel knew more about this than most modern Christians: "for we have heard him ourselves, and know that this is indeed the Christ, *the Saviour of the world*" (Jn. 4:42). Why did Christ give His flesh on the cross? The answer is for the life of the world (Jn. 6:33, 51).

Modernity encourages individualism, and consequently Christians relegate many of the passages to a type of solitary confinement. We don't think the cross was for the world, and we don't think there is enough power there to bring about another Christendom. But the atonement is not limited to the realm of individual salvation. "And he is the propitiation for our sins: and not for ours only, *but also for the sins of the whole world*" (1 Jn. 2:2). Propitiation is the averting or turning aside of wrath. God's wrath was upon our world for our sinfulness and in the cross Christ provided a propitiation for the entire world. Notice that God is attempting *nothing*—He is doing something. "The next day John seeth Jesus coming unto him, and saith, 'Behold the Lamb of God, which *taketh away* the sin of the world'" (Jn. 1:29). He does not *offer* to take away the sin; He takes it away.

The Church has been entrusted with a ministry of reconciliation, a ministry which has been greatly neglected in the last century. "To wit, that God was in Christ, reconciling the world unto himself, not imputing their trespasses unto them; and hath committed unto us the word of reconciliation" (2 Cor. 5:19; cf. Rom. 11:15). We are to carry on the ministry which was first entrusted to the apostles, and that is to proclaim the word of reconciliation. Now this is *committed* to us, *entrusted* to us. What can be said of unfaithful emissaries who tinker with the message? We no longer say that God actually reconciled the world to Himself, because we don't think that He did. We are honestly as full of unbelief at this point as the people we preach to.

Popular evangelicalism wants the atonement to touch every last man, woman, and child. But in order to get it to do so, the touch is made *ineffectual*. Pessimistic Calvinists want the touch to be effectual . . . for half a dozen people. But we are to preach an effectual cross, an efficacious cross which will manifest itself as nothing less than the salvation of the world. This salvation is appropriated *by faith*. "For the promise, that he should be the heir of the world, was not to Abraham, or to his seed, through the law, but through the righteousness of faith" (Rom. 4:13).

Our Lord Jesus Christ "was the true Light, which lighteth every man that cometh into the world" (Jn. 1:9). This means He is the Lord of Christendom as well.

The pagan world now sings in praise of the holy
standard of the Cross,
the entire earth trembles and in unison proclaims
the fame of the Cross, for in prayer it reveals
its inmost heart.

—Alcuin

CHAPTER 18

CONCLUDING UNMODERN POSTSCRIPT

The story of Christian culture is a story of incarnations. The Word became flesh to save the world. When Christian medievalism started living the Gospel, it started carving out truth, goodness, and beauty around the Mediterranean. It could do no less; it was delighting in the true and glorious God. Adoration bursts out in song and feast. Incarnations. We might say, then, that Christian culture is *the Gospel in bodily form*. It is what happens when we live the Gospel.

In this book, we've tried to sketch what the Gospel enfleshed looks like. We've tagged it "medieval Protestantism," but the label isn't essential. By pointing to medievalism (of all horrors!), we hoped to convey the size of the wild and radical shift needed to escape modernity's suffocating web. A mere side shuffle to postmodernism is hardly a wild departure from modernity. Modernity's web is so subtle and yet so powerful that postmodernists can't even perceive that they have yet to abandon the Enlightenment project they claim to abhor. More importantly, modernism has an even tighter and more invisible grip on contemporary, orthodox evangelicalism. Our every thought, word, and deed is tainted by Enlightenment categories, whether we're thinking about children, church, or charity. Medievalism presents a very real contrast to the idols of modern life. It takes very little to convince moderns that medievals lived in a different galaxy. We are so quick to believe all the modern lies about medievalism. Yet it's that very different medieval angle that allows us to see the normally invisible chains of modern life.

The sketch of Christian culture we've attempted in this book is by no means exhaustive. Even as we were going to print we continued to imagine new chapters that ought to be included. The discussion we settled on plays off the weaknesses and strengths of our own era. To lay it out somewhat unceremoniously, our chapters have traced the following foundational cultural features.

A healthy Christian culture would manifest:

- a love of beauty permeating every part of life
- a deep respect for the majesty and liberty of God
- a holy recognition of the deep biblical antithesis
- humility in covenantal redemption—imputed righteousness
- laughter as a habit of life
- a devotion to celebration—feasting and lovemaking
- the centrality of the Church
- a humble submission to godly tradition
- the peace of federal headship in marriage
- a soulful nurturing of children for millennia
- a community shaped by rural rhythms
- self-responsibility and a fading state
- an acknowledgment of creational hierarchies
- a harmony of gratitude and discipline in developing technologies
- the predominance of poetic over rationalistic knowledge
- a confidence in the triumph of the cross

This is the sort of culture that grows when we do something as simple as living the apostolic command to meditate on the true, good, and beautiful: "whatsoever things are true, whatsoever things are honest, whatsoever things are just, whatsoever things are pure, whatsoever things are lovely, whatsoever things are of good report; if there be any virtue, and if there be any praise, think on these things" (Phil. 4:8). This is the sort of culture that manifests when we have ears to hear: "whether therefore ye eat, or drink, or whatsoever ye do, do all to the glory of God" (1 Cor. 10:31).

Another way of seeing the simplicity of the Christian culture we've sketched is to see it as the manifestation of the fruit of the Spirit. The fruit of the Spirit shapes each of the discussions in this book. When we are individually and corporately devoted to "joy, peace, longsuffering, gentleness, goodness, faith, meekness, temperance" (Gal. 5:22–23), our communities will manifest medieval Protestantism. Such communities would stand out like a city on hill not for their perfectionistic legislation and humorless boycotts but for their mercy. They would be those to whom Christ will say, "for I was hungered, and ye gave me meat: I was thirsty, and ye gave me drink: I was a stranger, and ye took me in: Naked, and ye clothed me: I was sick, and ye visited me: I was in prison, and ye came unto me" (Mt. 25:35–36). To get there doesn't require anything political or intellectualistic or perfectionistic; it takes faith working through love (Gal. 5:6). And for that hope, we can rejoice in Christ's promise—Blessed are the meek; for they shall inherit middle earth.

BENEATH

Below the gray cathedral spire
The village lies in darkness,
Which few can come to penetrate.

Below the bright celestial fire
The path of earth is markless,
And leaves instead ethereal wake.

Below the highest heaven, higher
Than all the lesser dark, bless
All those who look in faith away.

Douglas Wilson

A MAN FROM UR

Before the sun, he leaves his tent, burying
a smile behind his hand, a laugh audible.
He sits in dark and presses stone, sharpening.
I know some show awaits that hill; holiness
awaits my line. He gazes up, countenance
a mirror of the stars; I see David there,
and there is Paul. Just left there shines Aúgustine,
King Alfred hunting beauty; and lord Charlemagne.
There Wycliffe weeps and slaughters rise, Huguenots.
I see them all, my boys and girls, dissonance
and harmony, Babylon and Christendom.
For *Puer natus est,* and He is righteousness.
I know too much to fear this day's sacrifice.
I cannot count these stars; So shall my seed be.
Let's go. My only Isaac sleeps, innocence
before some unknown miracle, visible.
But still too early, day is not. Vanity
of sleep on such a day! but rest Saint Abraham.

Douglas Jones